Stitch by Stitch

Volume 6

TORSTAR BOOKS

NEW YORK · TORONTO

Stitch by Stitch

TORSTAR BOOKS INC.
41 MADISON AVENUE
SUITE 2900
NEW YORK, NY 10010

Knitting and crochet abbreviations

approx = approximately
beg = begin(ning)
ch = chain(s)
cm = centimeter(s)
cont = continue(ing)
dc = double crochet
dec = decrease(e)(ing)
dtr = double triple
foll = follow(ing)
g = gram(s)
grp = group(s)
hdc = half double crochet

in = inch(es)
inc = increas(e)(ing)
K = knit
oz = ounce(s)
P = purl
patt = pattern
psso = pass slipped stitch over
rem = remain(ing)
rep = repeat
RS = right side
sc = single crochet
sl = slip

sl st = slip stitch
sp = space(s)
st(s) = stitch(es)
tbl = through back of loop(s)
tog = together
tr = triple crochet
WS = wrong side
wyib = with yarn in back
wyif = with yarn in front
yd = yard(s)
yo = yarn over

A guide to the pattern sizes

		10	12	14	16	18	20
Bust	in	32½	34	36	38	40	42
	cm	83	87	92	97	102	107
Waist	in	25	26½	28	30	32	34
	cm	64	67	71	76	81	87
Hips	in	34½	36	38	40	42	44
	cm	88	92	97	102	107	112

Torstar Books also offers a range of acrylic book stands, designed to keep instructional books such as *Stitch by Stitch* open, flat and upright while leaving the hands free for practical work.

For information write to Torstar Books Inc., 41 Madison Avenue, Suite 2900, New York, NY 10010.

Library of Congress Cataloging in Publication Data
Main entry under title:

Stitch by stitch.

Includes index.
1. Needlework. I. Torstar Books (Firm)
TT705.S74 1984   746.4   84-111
ISBN 0-920269-00-1 (set)

98765432

© Marshall Cavendish Limited 1985

Printed in Belgium

Contents

Crochet / COURSE 24

* Basket weave patterns
* Working basic basket weave
* Stitch Wise: more basket weave patterns
* Pattern for a bath mat

Basket weave patterns

Once you have mastered the basic crochet stitches and developed a fluent way of working, you'll be amazed at the variety of patterns and stitches you can work—some lacy, others dense and firm. A perfect example of the latter kind of texture is the group of basket weave patterns in this course. Each of them produces a lovely, bulky fabric with a heavily woven appearance.

Although it looks complicated, the basic basket weave pattern is not difficult to learn. You begin by working a row of double crochets; then on the following row you work around the *stem* of the next stitch, rather than under the top loop as you would normally do on a double crochet fabric. The woven effect is achieved by working either around the back of the stitch—which has the effect of pushing it forward—or around the front of the stitch—pulling it to the back. Blocks of stitches are usually worked alternately forward and then backward across the row, the position being reversed on the following row, so that the stitches at the back are brought forward and vice versa. The number of stitches in each block can vary, depending on the fabric you wish to make.

Working basic basket weave

The best way to discover how the fabric is made is to try it yourself. Start by making our sample, using a knitting worsted and a size G (4.50mm) hook. Our pattern uses blocks of 3 doubles and will therefore need a multiple of 3 chains, plus 2 extra for the turning chain (for the sample, 29 chains in all). If you wish, for example, to work 5 doubles in each block, you will need to make a multiple of 5 chains plus 2 extra turning chains.

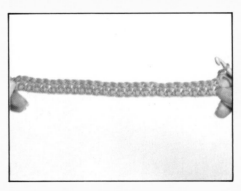

1 Work 1 row of doubles (27 in all). Now turn and make 2 chains. Since you are working around stem below top of stitch you need only make 2 chains instead of 3 as you would normally do when working a double crochet fabric.

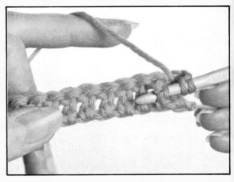

2 Wind the yarn over the hook and insert it around the back of the stem of the 2nd double, from right to left, taking the hook from the front of the work, through to the back and out to the front again, between the 2nd and 3rd doubles.

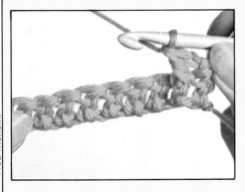

3 Wind the yarn over the hook, draw it through and complete the double in the normal way. You will see that this double has been pulled forward to the front of the fabric.

4 Now work 1 double around back of next double in same way to bring next stitch forward. Including first 2 chains, 3 stitches have now been worked to front, making a vertical section. This stitch is called "double around front."

5 Now begin the horizontal part of the pattern. Wind yarn over the hook, insert it from the back of the work, through to the front, around the stem of the next stitch to the left and through to the back of the work again.

Fred Mancini

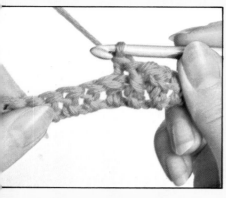

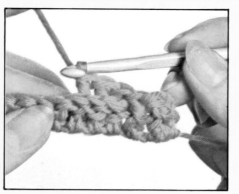

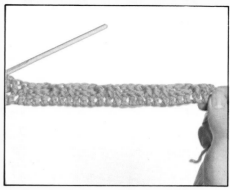

6 Now wind the yarn over the hook, draw it through the stitch, and complete the double in the normal way, so pulling this double to the back of the work. This method of working around the front of the stitch to bring it to the back is called "double around back."

7 Work 1 double in the same way around the front of the stem of each of the next 2 doubles, repeating steps 5 and 6 each time. Keep the hook at the back of the work while working these doubles.

8 Work the next 3 doubles to the front as before, repeating steps 2 and 3, then the next 3 doubles to the back, repeating steps 5 and 6 alternately across the row. Work last double to front, going around turning chain at end of row.

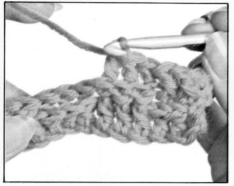

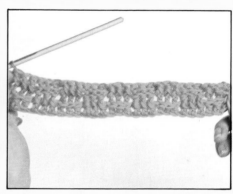

9 Turn and make 2 chains as before. The doubles which were at front on previous row now appear to be at back and vice versa. Skip first (edge) stitch and work each of next 2 doubles to front, repeating steps 2 and 3, so that they are now brought forward.

10 Now work each of next 3 doubles to the back, repeating steps 5 and 6, so that they are taken to back of work. You will see that the fabric is reversible.

11 Continue to alternate the position of the blocks of doubles across the row, so that each forward block is taken back and vice versa. Work last doubles around the turning chain in correct pattern sequence.

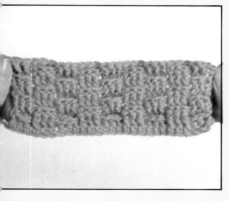

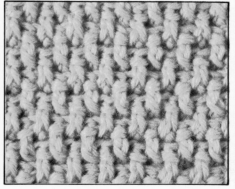

12 Work rows alternately in this way each time to create the woven effect. Several rows have been worked here, and you will see that where stitches have been worked to the back a ridge is formed running horizontally across fabric.

13 This sample shows blocks of 6 doubles worked in same way, but with 2 rows worked before alternating position, so that the forward stitches will be kept back on 2nd pattern row, before changing position on following row, to produce a strongly vertical pattern.

14 This sample shows the effect of working 1 double to the front and then one to the back all the way across the row. The position of the doubles is reversed each time on every row to produce this woven, lattice effect.

Fred Mancini

Stitch Wise

Although they are worked in different ways, these three patterns all suggest basket work in their textures.

Elongated basket stitch

Here you must work into the row two rows below, placing the hook between the stitches each time to make long doubles. The pattern is worked over a number of chains divisible by 6 plus 3, with 2 extra for the turning chain.

1st row 1dc into 4th ch from hook, 1dc into each ch to end. Turn.
2nd row 1 ch, skip first st, 1 sc into each st to end. Turn.
3rd row (WS) 3ch, skip first st, 1dc into each of next 2 sts, *(yo and insert hook between next 2 dc in row below, yo and draw yarn up to same height as row being worked, complete double in normal way—called 1dc below—3 times, 1dc into each of next 3 sts working in to top of stitch in normal way—called 1dc top—rep from * to end, working last dc into turning chain. Turn.
4th row (RS) As 2nd.
5th row 3ch, 1 dc below between first and 2nd dc in row below, 1 dc below between next 2dc, *1dc top into each of next 3sc, (1dc below between next 2dc) 3 times, rep from * to end, working last dc below between last dc and turning chain. Turn.
6th row As 4th.
3rd to 6th rows form pattern and are repeated throughout.

Basket weave variation

Unlike the basket weave stitches illustrated in the step-by-step photographs, this pattern has a definite right and wrong side to it. It is worked over a number of chains divisible by 10 plus 7, with 2 extra for the turning chain.

1st row (RS) 1dc into 4th ch from hook, 1dc into each ch to end. Turn.
2nd row 3ch, skip first dc, yo and insert hook from right to left from back to front, around stem of next dc and to back of work again, yo and draw through a loop, yo and draw through 2 loops yo and draw through rem 2 loops—1 double back; 1dcB around each of next 4dc, *1dc into each of next 5dc in normal way, 1dcB around each of next 5dc, rep from * to end, 1dc into top of turning chain. Turn.
3rd row 3ch, skip first dc, yo, insert hook between 2nd and 3rd, from front to back, around stem of next dc and to the front again, yo and draw through a loop, yo and draw through 2 loops on hook, yo and draw through rem 2 loops—1 double front, or 1dc F—around each of next 4dc, *1dc into each of next 5dc in normal way, 1dc F around each of next 5dc, rep from * to end, 1dc into top of turning chain. Turn.
4th row As 2nd.
5th row 3ch, skip first dc, 1dc into each of next 5dc in normal way, *1dcF around each of next 5dc, 1dc into each of next 5dc in normal way, rep from * to end, 1dc into top of turning chain. Turn.
6th row 3ch, skip first dc, 1dc into each of next 5dc in normal way, *1dcB around each of next 5dc, 1dc into each of next 5dc in normal way, rep from * to end, 1dc into top of turning chain. Turn.
7th row As 5th.
8th row As 6th.
9th row As 3rd.
10th row As 2nd.
The 3rd to 10th rows form pattern. Repeat them throughout until the fabric is the depth you want.

Raised double crochet pattern

Here doubles worked around the stem are worked alternately with doubles worked in the normal way to produce a highly textured, almost double fabric, similar in appearance to honeycomb stitch but made in squares, not diamonds. The pattern is worked over an uneven number of stitches. Begin by making an uneven number of chains.

1st row 1dc into 4th ch from hook, 1dc into each ch to end. Turn.
2nd row 3ch, skip first dc, *1dc around stem of next dc inserting hook from right to left from the front to the back and around to the front of the work again— 1 double front—1 dc into top of next st in normal way, rep from * to end, 1dc into top of turning chain. Turn.
3rd row 3ch, skip first dc, 1dc into top of next dc in normal way, 1dcF around next dc, rep from * to last 2dc, 1dc into next dc, 1dc into top of turning chain. Turn.
4th row As 2nd row, but ending with 1dcF, 1dc into top of turning chain. Turn.
5th row As 3rd.
4th and 5th rows form pattern and are repeated throughout. Note that you alternate the doubles on each row by working 1dcF into the normal double worked in previous row and vice versa each time. Continue in this way to the required depth.

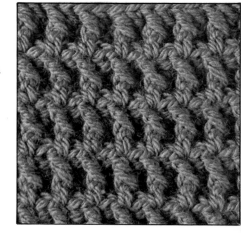

Mat finish

This bath mat is just the thing for catching splashes and drips. It is worked in a thick cotton yarn with a sturdy basket weave pattern and is trimmed around three sides with a short fringe.

Size
16in (42cm) by 26in (69cm), excluding fringe.

Materials
15oz (400g) of a medium-weight cotton yarn for mat; 4oz (100g) for fringe
Size E (3.50mm) crochet hook

Gauge
1 patt rep (12sts) to 2¼in (6cm) and 16 rows to 5in (13cm) in patt on size E (3.50mm) hook.

To make
Using size E (3.50mm) hook chain 140.
Base row 1dc into 4th ch from hook. 1dc into each ch to end. Turn.
Beg patt.

1st row (RS) 2ch, work *around* each of next 5dc by working yo, insert hook from front to back between next 2dc, around dc at left and through work from back to front; draw yarn through and complete dc in usual way—called double around front (dc around Ft), work *around* each of next 6dc by working yo, insert hook from back to front between next 2dc, around dc at left and through work from front to back; draw yarn through and complete dc in usual way—called 1 double around back (dc around Bk), now work *6dc around Ft, 6dc around Bk, rep from * to within last 6sts, dc around Ft to end. Turn.
2nd row 2ch, work 5dc around Bk, 6dc around Ft, *6dc around Bk, 6dc around Ft, rep from * to within last 6sts, dc around Bk to end. Turn.
3rd row As first row.

4th row As first row.
5th row As 2nd row.
6th row As first row.
These 6 rows form patt. Rep them 7 times more, then work first to 3rd rows again. Fasten off.

Fringe
Using four strands of yarn tog, knot fringe into every alternate row end along each short edge and into every alternate st along one long edge. Trim ends.

Crochet / COURSE 25

* Vertical chains worked on a crochet background
* Making the background fabric
* Working the vertical chains
* Pattern for a man's sleeveless sweater

Vertical chains worked on a crochet background

In this course we show you how to work crochet chains vertically onto a basic background fabric to make striped, checked and plaid patterns. These patterns are fun to work; you'll enjoy creating your own designs and using left-over pieces of yarn in imaginative ways. Remember, though, that before you start you must work out the sequence in which the colors are to be used, since you could otherwise end up with a haphazard and untidy-looking fabric.

You can either work the background in a plain color, using one or more contrasting colors for the vertical chains, or work it in a horizontal stripe pattern — again using contrasting colors for the chains — to create a more intricate pattern.

The fabric is worked in two stages. The first stage is to make a background, leaving spaces into which the chains can be worked. This can be an allover lattice pattern, in which case you will need to work the lines of chain evenly across the width of the fabric, filling in all the spaces. Or it can consist of blocks of double crochet interspersed with lattice pattern so that the crochet chains will only be worked at intervals across the fabric. The second stage is, of course, to work the lines of chain vertically up and down or across the fabric.

Making the background fabric

For the sample in steps 1-6 use a knitting worsted yarn and size F (4.00mm) hook.

1 Begin by making an uneven number of chains. Work 1 double into the 5th chain from the hook. (These 5 chains count as first double, skipped chain and 1 chain.) Make 1 chain. Skip next chain and work 1 double into next chain.

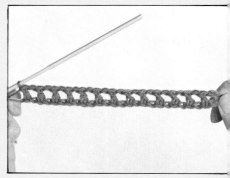

2 Now work 1 chain, skip next chain and work 1 double into next chain all the way across the row, working last double into last chain.

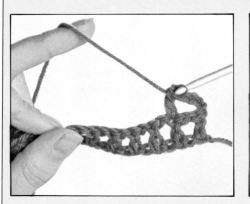

3 Turn and work 4 chains (to count as first double and 1 chain). Skip first (edge) double and space and work 1 double into next double.

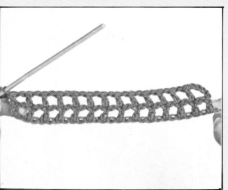

4 Continue to work 1 chain, skip 1 space and 1 double into next double all the way across the row. Work the last double into the 4th of first 5 chains to complete the row.

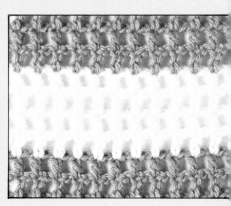

5 Continue to repeat steps 3 and 4, working last dc into 3rd of 4 chains, for each row of the lattice pattern. We used 2 colors for our sample, working 4 rows in each color throughout. Fasten off.

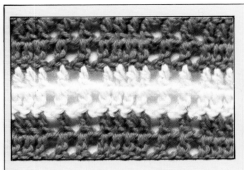

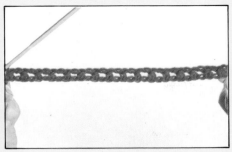

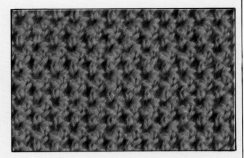

6 This sample shows a background fabric in which blocks of solid doubles and lattice stripes have been worked · alternately across the row. In this case 4 doubles have been alternated with 3 lattice spaces and worked in a striped pattern using two colors.

7 When using a sport yarn you may find it necessary to use half doubles in order to make the stitches the right proportion. A sport yarn worked in doubles will tend to produce a rather loose fabric. Half doubles will make a firmer fabric and will leave shorter spaces which can be more easily filled with chain. In this case, work the background as before, substituting half doubles for doubles throughout. You will have to begin with an uneven number of chains and work the first half double into the fifth chain from the hook.

8 On subsequent rows, work 3 chains to count as the first half double and 1 chain at the beginning of the row, instead of the 4 chains worked when using doubles for the background.

Working the vertical chains

The chain stitch used is essentially the same as that used in embroidery, even though it is worked with a crochet hook. Normally a double thickness of yarn is used for the chains.

You can either use two balls of yarn at the same time, or—if the piece that is to be covered is not very long—cut a piece approximately eight times the required length of the finished chain and fold it in half. (In this case you may not need to begin by making a slip knot, as in our sample, but can simply place the doubled yarn over the hook.)

1 Keep the RS of the background fabric facing you as you work. Make a slip knot on the hook, then insert the hook from front to back into the bottom right-hand corner space.

2 Wind the double yarn over the hook and draw it through the space and then through the loop on the hook. Always keep the ball of yarn at the back of the work.

3 Draw the loop up slightly and insert the hook from front to back into the next space. It is important to keep the yarn fairly slack when working each chain in order to avoid distorting the background fabric.

4 Repeat step 2 to complete this chain. Continue to work chains in this way all the way up the fabric, working into each space. Make the last chain over the top edge of the fabric and pull yarn through to fasten off. *continued*

Fred Mancini

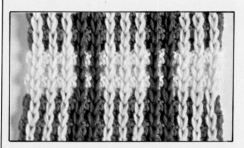

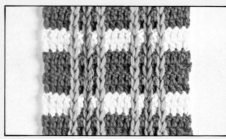

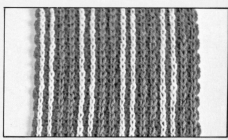

5 This sample shows each vertical line worked in chains, using one of the background colors and a contrasting color to create a simple check pattern. You will have to sew the loose ends of yarn to the WS of fabric when it is completed.

6 Here the background fabric previously worked, which combines blocks of doubles and lattice pattern, has been completed by working the vertical chain lines in two contrasting colors to achieve a plaid effect.

7 A single thickness of sport yarn has been used to make the chains on this sample, in which half doubles were used instead of doubles to create the background fabric. You will often find that you need to experiment with different-sized hooks and different background fabrics to obtain the desired effect in your chosen yarn. In some cases a single thickness of yarn works better than a double thickness.

Check mate

This smart sleeveless sweater is worked in half doubles. The fabric has contrasting horizontal stripes with vertical lines worked in chain.

Victor Yuan

Sizes
To fit 38[40:42:44]in (97[102:107: 112]cm) chest.
Length, 24¾[25¼:25½:25¾]in (63[64:65:66]cm).

Note Directions for larger sizes are in brackets []; if there is only one set of figures it applies to all sizes.

Materials
12[12:12:13]oz (325[325:325: 350]g) of a sport yarn in main color (A)
2oz (50g) in each of 2 contrasting colors (B) and (C)
Sizes C and E (3.00 and 3.50mm) hooks

Gauge
20 sts and 16 rows to 4in (10cm) in patt using size E (3.50mm) hook.

Back
**Using size E (3.50mm) hook and A, make 103[109:115:120]ch.
Base row 1hdc into 3rd ch from hook, 1hdc into each ch to end. Turn. 102[108:114:119] sts.
1st row (WS) 2ch to count as first hdc, 1hdc into each of next 10[13:13:16] hdc, *1ch, skip next hdc, 1hdc into each of

next 3hdc, 1 ch, skip next hdc, 1 hdc into each of next 20[20:22:22]hdc, rep from * twice more, 1 ch, skip next hdc, 1 hdc into each of next 3hdc, 1 ch, skip next hdc, 1 hdc into each of last 11[14:14:17]hdc. Turn.

2nd row 2ch, 1 hdc into each of next 10[13:13:16]hdc, *1 ch, 1 hdc into each of next 3hdc, 1 ch, 1 hdc into each of next 20[20:22:22]hdc, rep from * twice more, 1 ch, 1 hdc into each of next 3hdc, 1 ch, 1 hdc into each of last 11[14:14:17]hdc.

3rd-5th rows As 2nd row, but joining on B on last hdc of 5th row.

6th row Using B, work as 2nd row, cut off B, do not turn, but return to beg of row, so working in same direction as last row.

7th row RS facing and using A, work as 2nd row. Turn.

8th row As 2nd row, but joining on C on last hdc. Turn.

9th row Using C, work as 2nd row, cut off C, do not turn but return to beg of row.

10th row RS facing and using A, work as 2nd row. Turn.

11th-25th rows As 2nd row, but joining on B on last hdc of 25th row.

The 6th to 25th rows form patt. Cont

in patt until work measures 14½in (37cm) from beg.**

Shape armholes
Next row Sl st over first 5hdc, 2ch, patt to last 4hdc, turn.

Next row Sl st over first 3hdc, 2ch, patt to last 2hdc, turn. Work 2hdc tog (to dec one hdc) at each end of next 2[3:3:4] rows, then at each end of foll 2[2:3:3] alternate rows. 82[86:90:94]hdc. Cont straight until work measures 9½[10:10¼:10½]in (24[25:26:27]cm) from beg of armhole.

Shape shoulder
Next row Sl st over first 7[8:8:8]hdc, 2ch, patt to within last 6[7:7:7]hdc, turn. Rep this row twice more.

Next row Sl st over first 6[5:5:7]hdc, 2ch, patt to within last 5[4:4:6]hdc. Fasten off.

Front
Work as for back from ** to **
Shape armhole and divide for neck
Next row Sl st over first 5hdc, 2ch, patt 46[49:52:55]hdc, turn.
Work on this set of sts first.
Next row Dec 1hdc, patt to within last 2hdc, turn. Dec 1hdc at armhole edge on next and foll 1[2:2:3] rows, then on foll 2[2:3:3] alternate rows *and at same time* dec one hdc at neck edge on every foll alternate row until 23[25:25:27]hdc rem.
Cont straight until work measures

9½[10:10¼:10½]in (24[25:26:27]cm) from beg of armhole; end with WS row.

Shape shoulder
Next row Sl st over first 7[8:8:8]hdc, 2ch, patt to end. Turn.
Next row Patt to last 6[7:7:7]hdc. Turn.
Next row Sl st over first 7[8:8:8]hdc, 2ch, patt to end. Turn.
Next row Patt to last 5[4:4:6]hdc.
Fasten off. Rejoin yarn to rem sts at center front neck and complete to match first side reversing all shapings.

To work vertical chains
Make a slip knot on hook and work chain st up sp in patt as foll. Using B and keeping yarn at back of work insert hook into first sp and draw loop through, *insert hook into next sp, and draw loop through loop on hook, rep from * working fairly loosely up garment. Fasten off. Cont to work into all ch sp across row alternating B and C.

To finish
Press work with warm iron over damp cloth. Join shoulder and side seams. Using size C (3.00mm) hook and A finish edges as foll.
Neck: Work 4 rows of sc evenly around neck edge working (2sc tog) twice at center front on every row. **Armholes:** Work 4 rows of sc evenly around armhole. **Waistband:** Work 8 rows of sc evenly around lower edge.

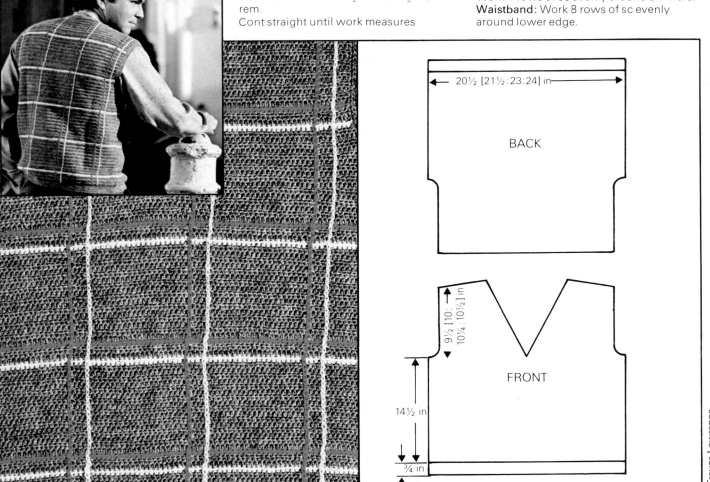

Trevor Lawrence

Shoestring

It's crazy!

This must be the easiest way to do patchwork—just cut out random shapes and stitch them together. You'll find the effect is fascinating.

Finished size
14in (36cm) diameter circle.
$\frac{5}{8}$in (1.5cm) seam allowances have been included throughout.

Materials

$\frac{5}{8}$yd (.5m) of 36in (90cm)-wide cotton print fabric
$\frac{1}{8}$yd (.2m) of 36in (90cm)-wide cotton fabric in each of two coordinating prints
$\frac{1}{2}$yd (.4m) of 36in (90cm)-wide cotton backing fabric
Two skeins of contrasting stranded embroidery floss
White sewing thread
$2\frac{3}{4}$yd (2.5m) of 2in (5cm)-wide eyelet lace edging
$1\frac{3}{4}$yd (1.5m) of narrow satin ribbon to match embroidery floss
14in (36cm)-diameter pillow form

1 From the largest piece of print fabric cut out a $15\frac{1}{4}$in (39cm)-diameter circle for the pillow back.
2 Cut a similar circle from backing fabric for pillow front.
3 From the three print fabrics cut out a variety of shapes: squares, triangles, etc.
4 Arrange these shapes on the front circle, overlapping their edges to cover the backing fabric underneath completely. Pin, baste and stitch all around the edge of each piece, using white sewing thread.
5 Using three strands of embroidery floss, work herringbone stitch around raw edges to finish and decorate.
6 Press the pillow front on the wrong side.
7 Join the ends of eyelet lace together to form a circle. Run a double line of gathering stitches along the raw edge of the eyelet lace edging.
8 Pin and baste the gathered eyelet lace to the right side of the patchwork front circle, raw edge outward, $\frac{5}{8}$in (1.5cm) from the outer edge, pulling up the gathers evenly to fit.
9 Pin, baste and stitch the pillow back to the patchwork circle, right sides facing, leaving a 10in (25cm) opening. Trim away excess fabric and clip curves. Turn pillow cover right side out. Press.
10 Insert pillow form. Turn opening edges under and slip stitch together to close.
11 Divide the ribbon into six equal pieces. Tie each piece into a bow. Sew each bow to the eyelet lace edging, at equally-spaced intervals.

Di Lewis

Crochet / COURSE 26

Hints on finishing

Sooner or later—and probably sooner—you will crochet a garment which involves detailed finishing. Many people think that once they have completed making all the separate pieces of a garment, the task is virtually finished, and that all they need to do is quickly sew the seams together. This, of course, is not true; careful pressing and seaming are essential if you want your garment to have a really professional finish. After all, you've probably spent a considerable amount of time and care in working the crochet. A few extra minutes at the finishing stage will make the difference between a sweater, jacket or dress which you'll be proud to wear and one that stays in the closet or drawer.

Blocking and pressing

If the pieces of your garment are to be pressed before seaming, you must first pin each piece to the correct size and shape on a flat, padded surface. This is known as "blocking." Some yarns can be pressed, and some cannot. On most ball bands you will find pressing directions. The ball band should also tell you whether the yarn should be wet or dry-pressed. Many man-made fibers need no pressing at all and can be ruined if they come into contact with heat, so check the ball band carefully before pressing. If you are in any doubt about how the yarn should be treated, it is better not to press it at all to avoid disappointment.

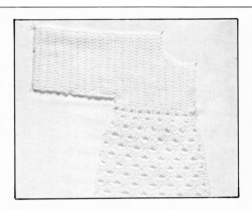

1 Place the piece to be pressed (RS down) on a flat, well-padded surface. A kitchen table covered with several layers of blankets and a sheet makes an ideal surface, since it is wider than an ironing board and provides plenty of room on which to lay the fabric out flat. Pin the piece at each corner as shown.

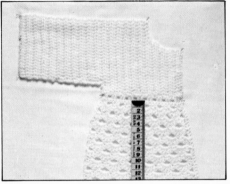

2 Now measure horizontally across the widest part and vertically down the center of the fabric to make sure that the measurements are the same as those given in the directions. If not, pat the fabric gently to the correct shape and size and pin once more at the lower edge.

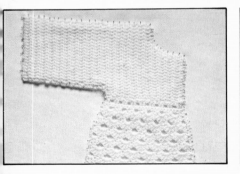

3 Now pin all around the fabric at intervals of about ¾in (2cm), taking care not to stretch the fabric, since this could result in a fluted edge. Check that corresponding sides measure the same and that stitches and rows are running straight before you begin to press.

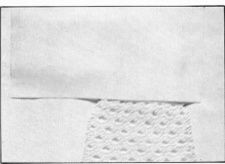

4 Place a clean cotton cloth (either damp or dry, depending on the type of yarn used) over the piece to be pressed. Remember that any ribbing on the garment should not be pressed, as this will flatten it, causing it to lose its elasticity.

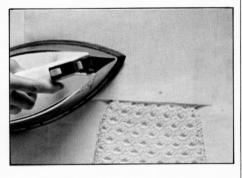

5 Pressing should always be done with a light touch, as over-pressing can easily ruin the soft, textured quality of crocheted fabrics. Set the iron at the correct temperature for the yarn, then press gently but firmly down on the cloth and lift the iron off again. Repeat this action all over the cloth, lifting and pressing, rather than pushing it over the cloth. Allow the fabric to cool before removing the pins.

Fred Mancini

Special cases

Highly textured patterns, such as cluster patterns, are normally not pressed, for pressing may destroy their distinctive appearance.

The same is generally true of lacy patterns. In some cases, however (usually when a natural fiber has been used), the pattern will instruct you to press the

garment lightly on the wrong side, taking care not to spoil the pattern.

First of all block the garment by pinning it on a padded surface as explained in the step-by-step instructions for blocking and pressing. Then take a clean damp cloth and lay it over the area to be pressed.

Hold the iron so that it just touches the cloth and leave it for a second or two. Repeat over the whole surface of the piece—except the ribbing, if any.

By pressing the wrong side of the fabric you will also be less likely to flatten textures in high relief such as bobbles.

Lightly textured fabric

A lightly textured fabric may simply be blocked and pressed around the edges, as shown here.

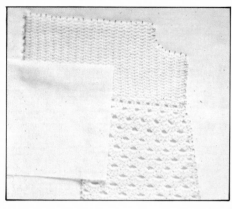

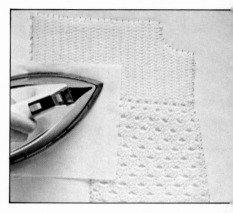

1 Block the piece to shape in the normal way, and then place a damp cloth over it.

2 Press around the edges only. This creates a firm edge, making it easier to sew the pieces together. Allow the fabric to cool completely.

Sewing the pieces together

To sew crocheted fabrics together use a blunt-ended yarn needle and the same yarn used for the garment. If this is too thick or unsuitable (a bouclé for example) you can substitute finer or more suitable yarn in a matching shade. Your directions will usually tell you in which order

the seams should be joined and the kind of seam to use for each piece. Remember that to avoid distorting the garment at the seams you must not draw the yarn too tightly through the fabric. Make sure that any patterns—such as shells or clusters—match exactly on each side of the seam

before sewing the pieces together. You can, in some cases, use single crochet to join the pieces together. This is usually worked on the right side of the fabric with a contrasting colored yarn to make a feature of the seam (see Crochet course 3, Volume 1, page 16).

Backstitch seam

This seam is generally used for the main parts of the garment, such as shoulder, side and sleeve seams, on fabric that is closely woven or textured, such as single crochet, half double or seed stitch fabrics. It creates a firm, strong seam ideal for sweaters and jackets.

1 Pin the two pieces to be joined with RS together. Work the seam approximately one crochet stitch in from the edge. Begin by making 2 small stitches on top of each other at the starting point of the seam to hold the yarn in place.

2 Insert the needle into the fabric again and bring it out slightly to the left of the fastening stitches. Now bring the needle to the right, insert it and bring it out a little farther to the left.

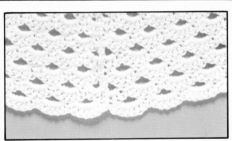

3 Continue to repeat step 2 all the way across the fabric, working in a straight line and inserting the needle where it emerged for the previous stitch, so that the stitches are all touching. Remember not to pull the yarn too tightly.

4 If you are using this seam at the shoulder, work in a straight line from the outer (armhole) edge to the inner (neck) edge, rather than following the steps created by the shoulder shaping.

5 If you had a set-in sleeve this could be sewn in first before joining the side and sleeve edges; these edges could then be joined in one continuous seam. This method produces a firm, neat seam as shown here.

Overcast seam

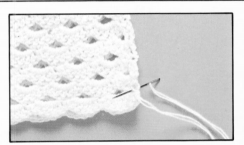

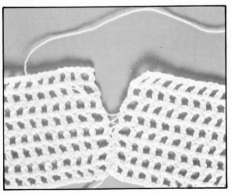

This is an ideal seam for ribbing or very open lace patterns, since it does not make a ridge on the fabric. The yarn is taken over the top of the edge and then passed through the edge stitches.

On lacy patterns, which may have more spaces than stitches along the edge—ruling out a backstitch seam—overcasting is a practical alternative, for you only need to pass the needle through the center of the chain or edge stitch to join the two pieces. Match any pattern on your fabric carefully on each side of the seam before joining the pieces together.

1 Place the two pieces with RS together. Using a blunt-ended needle and working from right to left make two small stitches at the beginning. With yarn at front of fabric pass the needle over the top of the two edges from front to back and insert the needle through the edges from back to front.

2 Now pull the yarn through firmly, but not too tightly, to complete the first stitch. Continue to work in same way across the fabric, working over the top each time until the seam is complete.

Invisible seam

Here is another method of seaming which is also well-suited to very open lace crochet fabrics, since you can just catch the stitches at either side of the seam, rather than having to work through the double thickness of fabric each time. Because the seam lies perfectly flat, with no hard ridges, it is also ideal for baby clothes, in which comfort is extremely important. Unlike the other seams it is worked with the pieces lying flat, RS up.

1 Place the two pieces of fabric edge to edge, RS facing up. Join the yarn to one side of the seam, taking 2 small stitches to secure it. Now take the yarn over to the other side and pass the needle under one stitch. If the fabric is particularly fine, you can pass the needle under 1 loop only of the stitch.

2 Take the needle back to the other side and under the next stitch on this side in the same way. Pull the yarn through firmly so that the stitch becomes invisible. Continue to work along the seam, catching one stitch at each side until the seam has been completed.

Fred Mancini

Stitch Wise

Diagonal shell pattern

This pattern is worked over a multiple of 8 chains plus 7 extra chains, and shows how simple shells and chain links can be worked in diagonal, rather than vertical lines. Make sure that you work the base chain loosely.

Base row (RS) 1sc into 3rd ch from hook, *5ch, skip 3ch, 1sc into next ch, rep from * to end of ch. Turn.

1st row 3ch to count as first dc, 2dc into first (edge) sc—called half shell—, 1sc into first 5ch loop, *5ch, 1sc into next 5ch loop, 5dc into next sc—called 1 shell—, 1sc into next 5ch loop, rep from * to end, ending last rep with 5ch, 1sc into top of turning chain. Turn.

2nd row 3ch to count as first dc, half shell into first sc, 1sc into next 5ch loop, *5ch, 1sc into center dc of next shell, 1 shell into next sc, 1sc into next 5ch loop, rep from * ending last rep with 1sc into top of turning chain. Turn.

3rd row 6ch, 1sc into first 5ch loop, *1 shell into next sc, 1sc into center dc of next shell, 5ch, 1sc into next 5ch loop, rep from * to end, ending with 1 shell into last sc, 1sc into top of turning chain. Turn.

4th row 6ch, 1sc into center dc of next shell, *1 shell into next sc, 1sc into next 5ch loop, 5ch, 1sc into center of next shell, rep from *, ending with 1sc into center dc of last shell, 1 shell into next sc, 1sc into 3rd of first 6ch. Turn.

5th row 3ch, half shell into first sc, 1sc into center dc of next shell, *5ch, 1sc into next 5ch loop, 1 shell into next sc, 1sc into center of next shell; rep from *, ending last rep with 5ch, 1sc into 3rd of first 6ch. Turn.

2nd to 5th rows form pattern and are repeated throughout.

For the little one

Make a jacket and matching bonnet for the newcomer in the family. The lacy pattern is highlighted by using a yarn with a shiny thread running through it.

Sizes

Jacket fits 18[19]in (46[48]cm) chest. Length, 11[12]in (28[30.5]cm). Sleeve seam, 4¾[5½]in (12[13.5]cm).

Note Directions for the larger size are in brackets []; where there is only one set of figures it applies to both sizes.

Materials

Jacket *4[5]oz (100[120]g) of a sport yarn*
Sizes E and F (3.50 and 4.00mm) hooks
3 buttons
1yd (1m) of ⅜in (1cm) ribbon
Bonnet *2oz (40g) of a sport yarn*
Size E (3.50mm) crochet hook
1yd (1m) of ⅝in (1.5cm) ribbon

Gauge

22 sts to 4in (10cm) and 22 rows to 5¼in (13cm) in yoke patt on size E (3.50mm) hook.

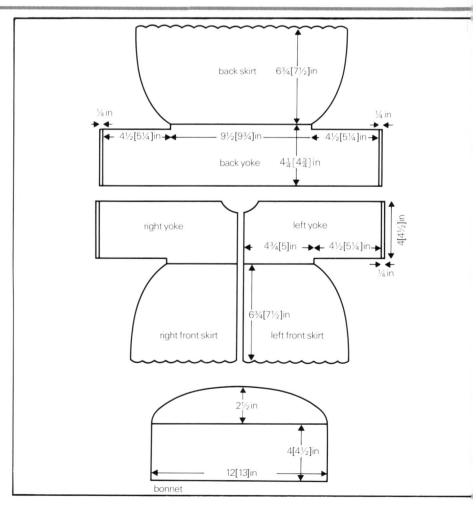

Jacket back yoke

Using size E (3.50mm) hook make 23[26] ch for left cuff.

Base row (WS) 1hdc into 3rd ch from hook, 1hdc into each ch to end. Turn. 22[25] sts.

Beg patt.

1st row 2ch to count as first sc, working into *back* loops only, work 1sc into each st to end. Turn.

2nd row 2ch to count as first hdc, 1hdc into each st to end. Turn.

Rep last 2 rows until work measures 4½[5¼]in (11.5[13]cm) from beg; end with 2nd patt row.

Next row Work 4ch for underarm, 1sc into 3rd ch from hook, 1sc into next ch, patt to end. Turn. 25[28] sts.

Cont in patt until work measures 14[15]in (35.5[38]cm) from beg; end with first patt row.

Next row Patt to last 3 sts, turn and leave last 3 sts for underarm. 22[25] sts.

Cont in patt until work measures 18½[20¼]in (47[51]cm) from beg; end with first patt row. Fasten off.

Left front yoke

Work as for back yoke until front measures 1 row less than back yoke to first underarm, so ending with a first patt row.

Fasten off.

Shape underarm

Next row Work 3ch, then patt across sts of sleeve. Turn.

Next row Patt across 22[25] sts, 1sc into each of next 3ch. Turn. 25[28] sts.

Cont in patt over all sts until front measures 3[3½]in (7.5[9]cm) from underarm; end with first patt row.

Shape neck

Next row Patt to last 5[6] sts, turn.

Dec one st at neck edge on next 3 rows. 17[19] sts. Work 4 rows without shaping. Fasten off.

Right front yoke

Using size E (3.50mm) hook make 18[20] ch. Work base row as for back yoke. 17[19] sts.

Next row (buttonhole row) 2ch, patt 1[2] sts, (2ch, skip 2 sts, patt 3 sts) 3 times, patt 0[1].

Work 2 rows in patt, then inc one st at neck edge on next 3 rows, so ending with a 2nd patt row. Fasten off.

Shape neck

Next row Work 5[6] ch, patt across sts of front. Turn.

Next row Patt to last 5[6] ch, 1hdc into each of next 5[6] ch. Turn. 25[28] sts.

Cont in patt until front measures 3[3½]in (7.5[9]cm) from end of neck shaping, end with first patt row. Fasten off.

Next row Skip first 3 sts for underarm, rejoin yarn to next st, 2ch, patt to end. Turn. 22[25] sts.

Cont in patt until front measures 4½[5¼]in

(11.5[13]cm) from underarm; end with first patt row. Fasten off.

Back skirt
Using size E (3.50mm) hook and with RS of work facing, work 50[56]sc across lower edge of back yoke. Turn.
**Next row (eyelet-hole row) 2ch, 1hdc into next st, *1ch, skip next st, 1hdc into each of next 2 sts, rep from * to end. Turn.
Next row 2ch, 1sc into each hdc and ch of previous row. Turn. 50[56]sc. Change to size F (4.00mm) hook. Beg patt.**
1st size only
Base row 2ch, 1sc into next st, *3ch, skip next st, 1sc into each of next 3 sts, rep from * to last 4 sts, 3ch, 1sc into each of last 2 sts. Turn.
2nd size only
Base row 2ch, 1sc into first st, *3ch, skip next st, 1sc into each of next 3 sts rep from * to last 3 sts, 3ch, skip next st, 1sc into each of last 2 sts. Turn.
Both sizes
***1st row 2ch, 1sc into next st, *5dc into 3ch sp, 1sc into center sc of 3sc, rep from * to end, finishing with 1sc into last st. Turn.
2nd row 2ch, *3ch, 1sc into each of center 3dc of group, rep from * to end, finishing with 2ch, 1dc into last st. Turn.
3rd row 3ch, 2dc into 2ch sp, *1sc into center sc of 3sc, 5dc into 3ch sp, rep from * to end, finishing with 2dc into 3ch sp, 1dc into last st. Turn.
4th row 2ch, 1sc into next dc, *3ch, 1sc into each of center 3dc of group, rep from * to end, finishing with 3ch, 1sc into each of last 2sts. Turn.
The last 4 rows form patt. Rep them 4 times more.
1st size only
Rep first row once more. Fasten off.
2nd size only
Rep first to 3rd rows inclusive once more. Fasten off.

Right front skirt
Using size E (3.50mm) hook and with RS of work facing, work 26[29]sc across lower edge of right front yoke. Work as for back skirt from **to**
1st size only
Base row Work as for back.
2nd size only
Base row 2ch, 1sc into next st, *3ch, skip next st, 1sc into each of next 3 sts, rep from * to last 3 sts, 3 ch, skip next st, 1 sc into each of last 3 sts. Turn.
Both sizes
Work as for back skirt from ***to end.

Left front skirt
Work as for right front skirt.

To finish
Press lightly on WS using a cool iron over dry cloth. Join shoulder and upper sleeve seams, then skirt and underarm seams.
Front and neck edging Using size E

(3.50mm) hook and with RS of work facing, work 1 row of sc up right front, around neck edge and down left front, working 3sc into each corner. Fasten off.
Using size E (3.50mm) hook and with RS of work facing, rejoin yarn to top of right front and work around neck edge as foll: 1ch, *1sc into each of next 2 sts, 3ch, sl st into first ch — picot formed, 1sc into next st, rep from * to top of left front. Fasten off.
Cuff edging Using size E (3.50mm) hook and with RS of work facing, work 36[42]sc around cuff edge. Join with a sl st into first sc.
2nd round Work in sc, dec 6 sts evenly.
3rd round Work picots as for neck edging. Fasten off.
Sew on buttons. Thread ribbon through eyelet holes to tie at front.

Bonnet
Using size E (3.50mm) hook make 68[74]ch. Work base row and patt 3 rows as for jacket back yoke. 67[73] sts. Beg patt.
Base row 2ch, 1sc into next st, *3ch, skip 3 sts, 1sc into each of next 3 sts, rep from * to last 5 sts, 3ch, skip 3 sts, 1sc into each of last 2 sts. Turn.
Cont in patt as for back skirt for 4[4½]in (10[11.5]cm); end with 2nd or 4th patt row.
Next row 1 ch, 1sc into each sc and ch of last row. Turn.
Work 3 more rows in sc.
Shape crown
1st row 2ch, 1sc into each of next 0[3]sts, (1sc into each of next 15 sts, work 2sc tog) 3 times, 1sc into each of next 15[18] sts. Turn. 64[70] sts.
2nd and every alternate row 1ch, 1sc into each st of previous row. Turn.
3rd row 2ch, 1sc into each of next 0[3] sts, (1sc into each of next 7 sts, work 2sc tog) 7 times, 1sc into each of next 0[3] sts. Turn. 57[63] sts.
5th row 2ch, 1sc into each of next 0[3] sts, (1sc into each of next 6 sts, work 2sc tog) 7 times, 1sc into each of next 0[3] sts. Turn. 50[56] sts.
7th row 2ch, 1sc into each of next 0[3] sts, (1sc into each of next 5 sts, work 2sc tog) 7 times, 1sc into each of next 0[3] sts. Turn. 43[49] sts.
Cont to dec in this way on every alternate row until 8[14] sts rem.
2nd size only
Next row (Work 2sc tog) 7 times.
Both sizes
Cut yarn, thread through rem 8[7] sts, gather up and fasten off securely.

To finish
Press as for jacket. Join seam as far as start of crown shaping.
Edging Using size E (3.50mm) hook and with RS facing, work one round of sc around front and neck edges. Fasten off.
Cut ribbon in half; make rosette at one end of each piece and sew to bonnet.

Shoestring

Decorate a pair of hair combs with floral-print flowers, buds and leaves to keep your hair prettily in place.

Flower combs

Materials

Two plastic hair combs
Small scraps of two floral print cotton fabrics
Small scraps of green cotton fabric
Harmonizing stranded embroidery floss
Flower stamens (available from notion departments)
Size 10 (1.00mm) steel crochet hook
Matching sewing threads
Tracing paper for patterns

1 For flowers, cut out two 2¼in (6cm) diameter circles from each floral print fabric. Place two different print circles with right sides together. Pin, baste and stitch close to the edge all around circles, leaving a small opening. Turn flower right side out, turn in opening edges and slip stitch together.

2 Take a small bunch of stamens and sew them securely to the center of the flower, gathering up the flower center slightly to give a wavy effect to the flower.
3 Repeat steps 1 and 2 to make the second flower.
4 Trace the pattern for the leaf. Cut out eight leaves from green cotton fabric. Place two leaves together with right sides facing. Pin, baste and stitch around curved edges. Turn leaf right side out, turn in straight lower edges and slip stitch together to close.
5 Using embroidery floss, work a line of stitches down the center of the leaf and then back again to fill in the spaces.
6 Repeat steps 4 and 5 to make four leaves.
7 Trace pattern for bud. Cut out two buds in floral print fabric. Cut out two

strips, each 1½ × 1in (4 × 2.5cm) from green cotton fabric. Fold one strip in half lengthwise with wrong sides together. Place folded strip to right side of one bud shape, along the straight edge, matching raw edges. Pin, baste and stitch along the straight edges. Fold the bud in half widthwise. Pin, baste and stitch around curved edges. Turn bud right side out. Turn in and gather up the remaining straight raw edges to give a puffed-up look.
8 Using embroidery floss, crochet a 1in (2.5cm) length of chain from the center back of bud.
9 Repeat steps 7 and 8 to make up the second bud.
10 Arrange two leaves, one flower and one bud on each comb. Sew each arrangement securely to the comb.

LEAF

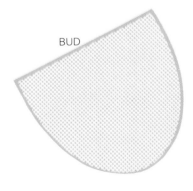

BUD

Crochet / COURSE 27

Making crochet braids

You can use crochet to make all sorts of interesting braids for trimming garments and household items. An enormous variety of yarns can be used this way, including cotton, colored string and chenille. Obviously, the range of colors and designs is much greater than you will find among ready-made trimmings, and the cost is considerably less.

At the end of this course we give directions for braid-trimmed boleros for mother and daughter but there are many other ways of using braid imaginatively. Try sewing crochet braids on pillows or curtains or around a bedspread in a coordinating shade. Very narrow braids can also be used as fastenings on jackets or coats. For a very simple narrow braid, twist one yarn around another while working a simple chain, perhaps using two different kinds or thicknesses of yarn. Wider braids can be embellished by threading ribbon through the center. Try working some of these braids in different yarns to see the variety of effects that are possible if you use your imagination.

Caterpillar braid

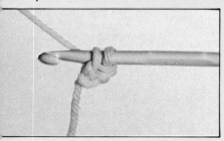 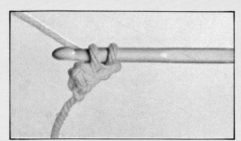 

1 Make 2 chains and work a single crochet into the first of these chains. Now twist the work in a half turn to the left (clockwise). Work a single crochet into the 2nd of the first two chains (the loop at the top of the work), inserting the hook from right to left through the loop when beginning the sc.

2 After completing the first sc, turn the work again in a clockwise direction and work the next single crochet into the first of the two loops which come over the top of the braid.

3 Continue to turn the braid each time after working the single crochet into the top loop, until the piece is the length you want. Or, make a bulkier braid by placing the hook through both the top loops instead of just the one at the top. Complete the braid by drawing the yarn through all 3 loops at once when working the last single crochet.

Ring braid

This attractive braid is made by working consecutive crochet rings and working single crochet into each ring on one side only, then turning and working back along the other side of each ring the same way to complete the braid. It can be made to any length, and by altering the number of chains worked each time, you can change the size of the rings, too.

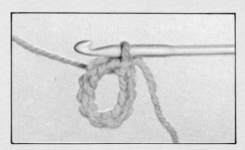 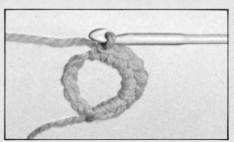

1 Make 12 chains. Remove hook from working loop and insert it into the first of these chains from front to back. Now pick up the working loop again and draw it through the first chain to make the first ring.

2 Now work 8 single crochet over one side of the ring, working from right to left, thus making the first side of the first ring—be careful not to twist the chain circle when you work the single crochets.

continued

Fred Mancini

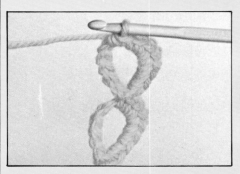

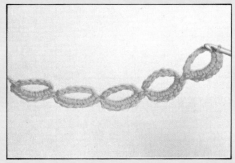

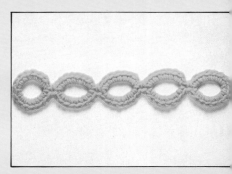

3 Make another 12 chains. Remove the hook from the working loop and insert it into the first of these chains. Pick up the working loop again and draw it through the first loop to form the 2nd ring. Work 8 single crochets into this ring in the same way as for first ring.

4 Continue to work a series of rings and single crochets in this way until the braid is the length you need. Now turn the braid so that the unworked side of the rings is uppermost and the hook is on the right.

5 Work back along this side of the braid, making 8 single crochets into each ring and 1 single crochet into the loop between the rings. Join the last single crochet to the first with a slip stitch to complete the first ring neatly. Fasten off.

Crescent braid

This pretty braid is worked over a small number of basic chains, turning the work each time to achieve the double-sided scalloped effect. You could vary the effect by threading narrow ribbon through the center.

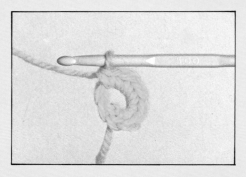

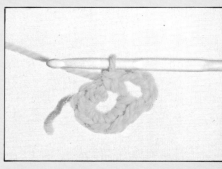

1 Make 5 chains and insert the hook into the first chain. Draw this chain through the working loop to form a circle. Now work 6 single crochets into the center of the circle as you would when working a circular motif.

2 Next, work 4 chains and then another single crochet into the circle in the same way. Turn the work so that the 4 chains just worked are at the beginning of the row.

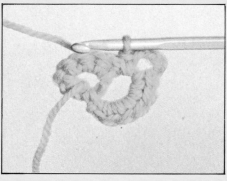

3 Now work 6 single crochets into this 4-chain loop to begin the second crescent shape on the other side of the braid.

4 Work 4 chains and then work 1 more single crochet into the same 4-chain loop. This completes the shape on this side.

5 Now turn and repeat steps 3 and 4 into the last chain worked. Continue to work in this way, repeating from step 3 each time. Finish the braid by working 6 single crochets into the last 4-chain loop; then work a slip stitch to neaten the end of the braid and fasten off the yarn.

Woven braid

This unusual braid is taken from Tunisian or Afghan crochet, in which all the loops are first worked onto a special long hook and then worked off it again without turning the work at the end of each row. We have made a narrow braid which can be worked with an ordinary crochet hook. You can vary the width of the braid by altering the number of chains you begin with, but don't make it too wide as you will find it difficult to work a large number of stitches on and off the hook. (Tunisian crochet techniques will be covered thoroughly in Volumes 14 and 15.)

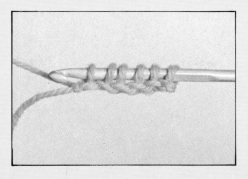

1 Begin the braid with 6 chains. Insert the hook into the 2nd chain, making sure that you place the hook under two loops in the base chain to make a firm edge. Wind the yarn over the hook and draw through a loop. Work thus into each chain so that you finish with 6 loops on hook.

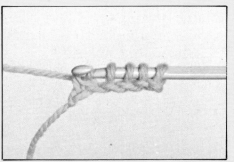

2 Don't turn the work as you would normally do at this point, but work back along the row from left to right. Wind the yarn over the hook and draw it through the first loop on the hook. Then wind the yarn over the hook and draw it through the next 2 loops.

3 Continue to work 2 loops off each time until only the working loop remains on the hook. Once again, you should not turn the work, but continue to work back along this row from right to left.

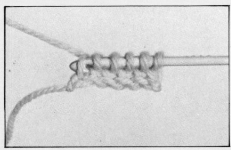

4 Insert the hook so that it passes behind the 2nd vertical loop at the front of the work, and draw through a loop. Continue to insert the hook behind each vertical loop, working the last loop by passing the hook behind the last vertical loop at the edge of the braid and drawing a loop through as before.

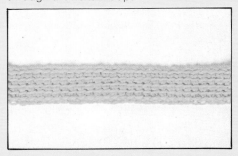

5 Continue to work the loops off and then onto the hook in this way each time, without turning the work, until the braid is the length you need. Fasten off.

Fred Mancini

Stitch Wise

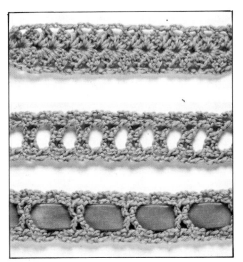

Shell stitch braid

Simple shells worked in a narrow strip make this attractive braid. Try working it in fine crochet cotton as an alternative to the knitting worsted used here. Make 4 chains and join the last chain to the first with a slip stitch.
1st row 3ch, 3dc into center of circle, 2ch, 4dc into circle. Turn.
2nd row 3ch, 3dc into 2ch loop, 2ch, 3dc into same 2ch loop, 1dc into top of turning chain. Turn.
The 2nd row forms the pattern. Repeat it for the length of braid required.

Buttonhole braid

This braid can be used either as it is or with ribbon threaded through the center. It is worked over a small number of basic chains for the width of the braid. If you wanted a wider strip you could work two widths side by side. Make 11 chains.
1st row 1dc into 4th chain from hook, 2ch, skip 2ch, 1sc into next ch, 2ch, skip 2ch, 1dc into each of next 2ch. Turn.
2nd row 3ch, skip first dc, 1dc into next dc, 5ch, 1dc into next dc, 1dc into top of turning chain. Turn.
3rd row 3ch, skip first dc, 1dc into next dc, 2ch, 1sc into 5ch loop, 2ch, 1dc into next dc, 1dc into turning chain. Turn.
The 2nd and 3rd rows form pattern and are repeated for the length required.

Border lines

Imaginative use of braid gives contrasting color and texture to these bright boleros.

Sizes

To fit 24[26:28:30:32:34:36:38]in (61[66:71:76:83:87:92:97]cm) chest/bust.
Length, 12¼[13:15½:16¼:17¾:19:20½: 21¼]in (31[33:37:41:45:48:52:54]cm).

Note Directions for larger sizes are in brackets [ ]; where there is only one set of figures it applies to all sizes.

Materials

5[5:6:6:7:7:9:9]oz (120[120:160: 160:200:200:240:240]g) of a sport yarn in main color (A)
2[2:2:2:3:3:3:3]oz (40[40:40:40:80: 80:80:80]g) in first contrasting color (B)
2oz (40g) in second contrasting color (C) for 3 color version
Sizes E and F (3.50 and 4.00mm) hooks

Gauge

17hdc and 14 rows to 4in (10cm) on size F (4.00mm) hook.

Main part (one piece to armholes)

Using size F (4.00mm) hook and A, make 113[121:131:141:147:155:165:175]ch for entire lower edge.
Base row (RS) 1hdc into 3rd ch from hook, 1hdc into each ch to end. Turn. 112[120:130:140:146:154:164:174] sts.
Patt row 2ch to count as first hdc, 1hdc into each hdc to end, working last hdc into top of turning ch. Turn. This row forms patt. Cont in patt for 7[7½:8½:9½: 10¼:11:12¼:12½]in (18[19:21.5:24.5:26: 28:31:32]cm).

Divide for armholes

Next row 2ch, 1hdc into next 21[22:23: 24:25:26:27:28]hdc, turn. Cont on these sts for right front until work measures 10¼[10¾:12¼:13¾:15:16¼:17¼:17¾]in (26[27:31:35:38:41:44:45]cm) from beg; end at inner edge.

Shape neck

Next row 2ch, 1hdc into each of next 9sts, turn. Cont on these sts until work measures 12¼[13:14½:16¼:17¾:19:20½: 21¼]in (31[33:37:41:45:48:52:54]cm) from beg. Fasten off. With RS facing skip next 12[14:17:20:20:22:24:27]sts for armhole, rejoin yarn to next st and work 2ch to count as first hdc, 1hdc into next 43[45:47:49:53:55:57:59]sts, turn and work on these sts for back until work

Serge Krouglikoff

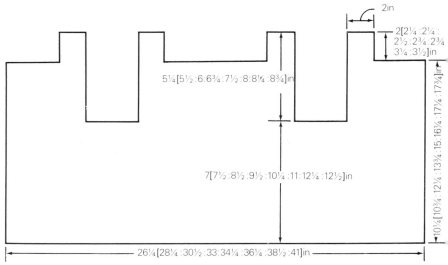

5¼[5½:6:6¾:7½:8:8¼:8¾]in

2[2¼:2¼: 2½:2¾:2¾: 3¼:3½]in

7[7½:8½:9½:10¼:11:12¼:12½]in

26¼[28¼:30½:33:34¼:36¼:38½:41]in

2in

10¼[10¾:12¼:13¾:15:16¼:17¼:17¾]in

measures same as right front up to neck shaping; end with RS row.

Shape neck
Next row 2ch, 1hdc into next 9sts, turn. Cont on these sts until work measures same as side of neck on right front. Fasten off. Skip next 24[26:28:30:34:36: 38:40]sts, rejoin yarn to next st and work 2ch, 1hdc into each st to end. Turn. Work to match first side of neck. With RS facing skip next 12[14:17:20:20:22: 24:27]sts for armhole, rejoin yarn to next st and complete to match right front reversing shaping. Fasten off.

To finish
Join shoulder seams. Using size F (4.00mm) hook and B, work sc around outer edge of bolero, do not turn but work row of crab st (sc worked from left

to right). Fasten off. Finish armhole edges in same way.

Braids for sizes 24[26:28:30]in (61[66: 71:76]cm) only (in 3 colors)
Using size E (3.50mm) hook and B make 4ch. Following directions on page 23 make a length of woven braid to fit along lower edge and 2 more lengths to fit along each front edge between lower braid and front neck.
Using size F (4.00mm) hook and C, make 12ch. Following directions on page 21 make a length of ring braid to fit all around bolero. Using size F (4.00mm) hook and B, make 2ch. Following directions on page 21 make a length of caterpillar braid to fit all around bolero. Using size F (4.00mm) hook and C make 5ch. Following directions on page 22 make a length of crescent braid to fit all

around bolero. Position braids on bolero and sew in place.

Braids for sizes 24[26:28:30]in (61[66: 71:76]cm) only (in 2 colors)
Work lengths of ring, caterpillar and crescent braid as for 3 color bolero but use B throughout. Position braids on bolero and sew in place.

Braids for sizes 32[34:36:38]in (83[87: 92:97]cm) only Using size E (3.50mm) hook and B, make 9ch.
Base row 1dc into 4th ch from hook, 4ch, skip next 3ch, 1dc into each of last 2ch. Turn.
Next row 3ch to count as first dc, 1dc into next dc, 4ch, 1dc into next dc, 1dc into turning ch. Turn.
1st row 3ch, 1dc into next dc, 2ch, insert hook under first 4ch loop from back to front, work 1sc around 2 loops at center to draw them tog,—called 1sc around ch, 2ch, 1dc into each of last 2dc. Turn.
2nd and 3rd rows 3ch, 1dc into next dc, 4ch, 1dc into each of last 2dc. Turn. These 3 rows form patt. Cont in patt until braid fits along lower edge of bolero, with even number of holes. Make 2 more lengths for each front edge from top of braid to neck edge. Join one short edge of each front braid to lower braid, then work row of sc around inner edge. Do not turn but work row of crab st (sc worked from left to right). Fasten off. Position braids on bolero and sew in place.

Shoestring

Tommy string bag

LEAVES

Colorful Tommy Tomato holds a ball of string neatly. He also hangs up so the string is close at hand.

Finished size
About 7½in (19cm) in diameter.

Materials
*Piece of red felt 16in (40.5cm) square
Piece of green felt 8½ × 5½in (22 × 14cm)
4in (10cm) square of white felt
2¼in (6cm) square of black felt
Black stranded embroidery floss
Brown soft embroidery thread
Matching thread; fabric glue
Paper for pattern
Tracing paper for patterns*

1 For main tomato piece, cut out a 7½in (19cm) diameter circle from paper. To make top edge, cut straight across one side of the circle, ¼in (6mm) from edge, and discard.
2 Cut out two main tomato pieces from red felt.
3 From black felt cut out four 1¼in (3.5cm)-diameter circles for pupils. From white felt cut out four ¼in (6mm)-diameter circles for highlights. From white felt cut out four 1½in (4cm) squares for outer eyes. Round off two corners of each.
4 Glue the highlights to the pupils and the pupils to the outer eyes. Glue the complete eyes to each tomato piece.
5 Using six strands of embroidery floss and working in stem stitch, embroider two eyebrows, a nose and a mouth on each tomato piece.
6 Place together with wrong sides together. Pin, baste and blanket stitch all around the edge, leaving top straight edges open.
7 Trace pattern for leaves. Cut out two of each size from green felt. Pin, baste and stitch the leaves together in pairs and then to the center of top straight edge on each side of the tomato.
8 Cut two 8½in (22cm) pieces of soft embroidery thread. Knot one end of the first piece. Thread this along top straight edge from one center around to opposite center. Repeat with second piece of soft embroidery thread.
9 Knot both pieces of soft embroidery thread together in the middle. Insert the ball of string, pull up the ties and hang.

Kim Sayer

26

* Three-dimensional flower motifs
* Crocheted rose
* Simple primrose
* Stitch Wise: Pineapple square
* Pattern for a bedspread

Three-dimensional flower motifs

In this course we show you one of the most intriguing and unusual crochet techniques: working a three-dimensional flower motif. The flowers are most frequently worked as part of a crochet square such as the granny square featured in Crochet course 12 (Volume 3, page 9), but they can be worked as separate motifs and sewn on any crocheted or knitted fabric; they can also be sewn on clothes as well as household items.

Today, these flowers are usually worked in a knitting yarn or fairly thick cotton yarn, and used to decorate bedspreads, rugs or elaborate shawls, but in the past they were more often worked with a fine steel crochet hook in very fine crochet cotton and used on baby clothes, lingerie and fine lace collars. Such very fine crochet was particularly fashionable in the middle and late 19th century, when people were accustomed to spending long hours patiently doing intricate needlework.

Crocheted rose

These step-by-step directions show you how to work the beautiful rose featured on the bedspread at the end of this course. In our sample—as in the bedspread pattern—the layers of petals are worked in different colors, but you could, of course, use just one color.

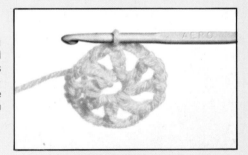

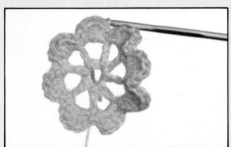

1 Begin flowers with 6 chains; join them into a circle with a slip stitch. The first round is made by working 1 double and 2 chains into circle 8 times, thus making 8 center "ribs" of flower. First, make 5 chains; these chains will count as first double and 2-chain space. Continue to work 1 double and 2 chains around circle, 7 more times. Finish round by joining last chain to 3rd of 5 chains with a slip stitch.

2 For the second round work 1 single crochet, 1 half double, 3 doubles, 1 half double and 1 single crochet into each 2-chain space of the previous round. Each of these groups of stitches forms a petal. Complete the round by using a slip stitch to join the last stitch to the slip stitch worked at the end of the previous round.

3 The next round consists of chains linking the petals already worked; the chains are joined to the petals with single crochet. Begin by making 4 chains. Now insert hook from back to front and around stem of first double worked in first round and work a single crochet in the normal way.

4 Keeping the 4 chains at the back of the petals all the time, work 4 chains and then a single crochet around the next double in the first round all the way around the flower. Complete the round by working 4 chains and joining this with a slip stitch to the first chain at the beginning of the previous round.

5 Some patterns instruct you to turn the flower so the WS faces you when working the chains. In this case work the single crochets around the stem of the stitch worked in the previous round, then turn flower to RS again before you work the petals. Here we show the back of the flower with linking chains worked in a contrasting color.

continued

Fred Mancini

6 Now work a petal into each of the chain loops worked in the previous round. You should work 5 doubles instead of the 3 worked in the previous petal round to increase the size of these petals. Use a slip stitch to join the last single crochet of the last petal to the first. The flower now has two layers.

7 Now work chain loops in exactly the same way as for the 3rd round, but work the single crochet linking each 4-chain loop around the back of the single crochet which you worked in the 3rd round. This has the effect of pulling the flower together at the back.

8 Work another round of petals into these chain loops as before, but this time work 7 doubles instead of 5 to make yet larger petals. If you need to make a smaller flower than the one we have made, you could finish the flower with this round.

9 Work another round of linking chains as before, working the single crochet around the back of the single crochet worked in the 5th round. Complete the flower with a final layer of petals, working 1 single crochet, 1 half double, 2 doubles, 5 triples, 2 doubles, 1 half double and a single crochet for each petal.

10 The flower is now complete. You can use it by itself by sewing it on any fabric. Or, enlarge the motif, giving it a granny-square type of background, as shown here.
Begin by working the chain loops as before at the back. Work 3 doubles, 3 chains, and 3 doubles into first loop for corner. Work 1 chain, 3 doubles and 1 chain into next loop. Repeat alternately into each loop to make 4 corners.

11 On subsequent rounds you will work a corner into each 3-chain space, and a 3-double crochet into each 1-chain space with 1 chain at either side, so that on each round you will be increasing a block of doubles on each side of the square. You can continue in this way until the square is as big as you require.

Simple primrose

Here is a much simpler flower which can also be worked with the same background. We have worked only two layers of petals, but you could make more for a larger flower.

1 Make 6 chains and join them into a circle with a slip stitch, as you would when working a square or circular motif. Now begin the first petal by working 1 single crochet, 3 doubles and 1 single crochet all into the center of the ring.

2 Make 2 more petals in exactly the same way and finish the round by joining the last single crochet to the first with a slip stitch. If you are using more than 1 color, fasten off the yarn at this stage by drawing it through the working loop. Make sure that this yarn is kept at the back of the work on following rounds.

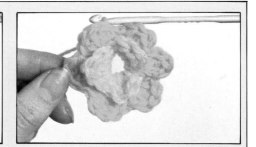

3 Turn the flower over so that the WS is facing you and rejoin the yarn to the back of the first single crochet. Make 3 chains and then work a single crochet into the back of the 2nd (middle) double of the first petal, passing the hook behind the 2 back loops.

4 Make 3 more chains and work a single crochet around the stem of the first single crochet in the 2nd petal. Continue to work 3 chains and a single crochet in this way all the way around the flower so that you finish with six 3-chain loops in all. Join the last chain to the first with a slip stitch to complete the round.

5 Now turn the flower back so that the RS is facing you. (Cut off yarn here if you wish to change color and rejoin it to first loop.) Now work a petal into each of the 6 loops in exactly the same way as before. If you wish to make more layers, make another round of chain loops and work into these loops. You may have to increase the size of the petals by working 5 doubles instead of 3.

6 To begin the background turn the flower to the WS again and work a 3-chain loop between each petal, linking the chains by working a single crochet around the stem of the single crochet worked in the previous loop round. You should have 6 loops in all.

7 Now turn the flower to the RS again and make 3 chains for the double. Now work 2 doubles, 2 chains and 3 doubles all into the first loop. Make 1 chain and work 3 doubles, 2 chains and 3 doubles into each loop all the way around, with 1 chain between each loop, joining the round with a slip stitch.

8 To make the square, either slip stitch across to the first 2-chain space, if you are using the same color, or join in a new color to this space. Make 3 chains to count as first double, then work 2 doubles, 3 chains and 3 doubles into first space. Work blocks of 3 doubles into the two spaces, linked by 1 chain. Work another corner of 3 doubles, 3 chains and 3 doubles. This sets the pattern.

Fred Mancini

Stitch Wise

Pineapple square

The flower motif in the center of this bulky pineapple stitch square is worked into the middle of the square after the square has been completed. By alternating a square with a flower and one without, you could make a very pretty bedspread or afghan.

Make 8 chains and join into a circle with a slip stitch.
1st round *(Yo and insert hook into circle, yo and draw up a loop) 4 times, yo and draw it through all 9 loops on hook, called pineapple 4, 2ch; rep from *7 times more. Join last chain to first pineapple with sl st. 8 pineapples.
2nd round Pineapple 4 into 2ch sp before sl st, *2ch, pineapple 4 into next sp, 2ch, (1dc, 3ch, 1dc) into top of next pineapple

st, 2ch, pineapple 4 into next sp; rep from *, ending last rep with (1dc, 3ch, 1dc) into next sp, 2ch. Join last ch to first pineapple with sl st.
3rd round Pineapple 4 into sp before sl st, *(2ch, pineapple 4) into each sp to corner, 2ch, (1dc, 3ch, 1dc) into corner; rep from * to end, 2ch. Join last ch to first pineapple with sl st.
Rep 3rd round for the size of square required.

To make the flower
Rejoin yarn to a 2ch sp on first round. Make 2ch to count as first sc, (yo and insert hook into same sp, draw up loop) 3 times, yo and draw through loops on hook, (pineapple 3), 1ch, pineapple 3 in same sp, 1ch, 1sc in same sp, *(1sc, pineapple 3, 1ch, pineapple 3, 1ch, 1sc) all into next 2ch sp in first round; rep

from * all around motif. Join last sc to first with sl st. Fasten off.
There should be 8 petals in all.

This pretty throw bedspread is just the thing for a young girl's bedroom. Or use it to bring a splash of color to your guest room. The edges of the motifs are given gentle emphasis by being joined with pink yarn. If pink does not go with your color scheme, make it in shades of yellow and gold.

We have laid a white sheet under the bedspread, but for extra color you could use a pink sheet. If you prefer, line the bedspread. Only the flat section needs to be lined; for this you will need 2½yds (2.3m) of 45/47in (115/120cm)-wide fabric.

Everything's coming up roses

This splendid bedspread with its three-dimensional rose motifs will appeal to a romantic nature. The rose motifs are alternated with plain motifs and the border is worked in rounds using each of the colors.

Size
To fit a twin bed—64in (163cm) by 90in (230cm) approx.

Materials
Knitting worsted yarn:
31oz (860g) in main color (A)
12oz (340g) in first contrasting color (B)
12oz (340g) in 2nd contrasting color (C)
8oz (200g) in 3rd contrasting color (D)

Size F (4.00mm) crochet hook

Gauge
One motif measures 7½in (19cm) square.

Rose motif
Using size F (4.00mm) hook and B, make 6ch, join with sl st to first ch to form ring.
1st round 3ch to count as first dc, *2ch, 1dc into ring, rep from * 6 times more, 2ch, join with sl st to 3rd of first 3ch.
2nd round Work 1sc, 1hdc, 3dc, 1hdc and 1sc all into each 2ch sp, join with sl st to

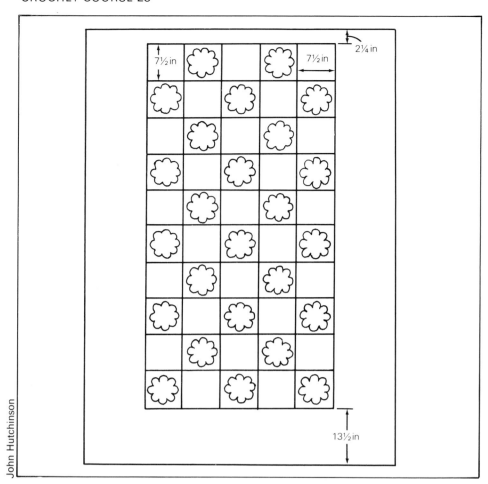

In the diagram:
- 7½ in
- 7½ in
- 2¼ in
- 13½ in

John Hutchinson

sl st at end of first round.

3rd round Keeping each 4ch loop behind petals of 2nd round, work *4ch, placing hook from back to front work 1sc around next dc on first round, rep from * 6 times more, 4ch, join with sl st to sl st at end of previous round.

4th round Work 1sc, 1hdc, 5dc, 1hdc and 1sc all into each 4ch loop, join with sl st to sl st at end of 3rd round.

5th round As 3rd round working into back of sc of 3rd round. Cut off B.

6th round Join C to sl st at end of last round, work 1sc, 1hdc, 7dc, 1hdc and 1sc all into each 4ch loop, join with sl st to sl st at end of 5th round.

7th round As 3rd round working into back of sc of 5th round.

8th round Work 1sc, 1hdc, 2dc, 5tr, 2dc, 1hdc and 1sc all into each 4ch loop, join with sl st to sl st at end of 7th round. Cut off C.

9th round Join D to center tr of one petal, 1ch to count as first sc, then work 7ch, *keeping last loop of each on hook work 3tr into center tr of next petal, yo and draw through all 4 loops on hook—called cluster 1 or Cl 1—, 4ch, Cl 1 into same st as last Cl 1, 7ch, 1sc into center tr of next petal, 7ch, rep from * twice more, work Cl 1, 4ch and Cl 1 all into center tr of next petal, 7ch, join with sl st to first ch. Cut off D.

10th round Join A to one corner 4ch sp, 3ch to count as first dc, 2dc into corner sp, 3ch, 3dc into same sp, 1ch, *(3dc, 1ch, 3dc and 1ch all into next 7ch sp) twice, 3dc, 3ch, 3dc and 1ch all into corner 4ch sp, rep from * twice more, (3dc, 1ch and 3dc all into next 7ch sp) twice, join with sl st to 3rd of first 3ch.

11th round Sl st over 2dc and into 3ch sp, 3ch to count as first dc, 2dc into sp, 3ch, 3dc into same sp, (1ch, 3dc into next 1ch sp) 5 times, * 1ch, 3dc, 3ch and 3dc all into corner 3ch sp, (1ch, 3dc into next 1ch sp) 5 times, rep from * 3 times, 1ch, sl st into 3rd of first 3ch.

12th round As 11th round but working six 3dc clusters between each corner. Fasten off.
Make 24 more motifs in same way.

Plain motif
Using size F (4.00mm) hook and A, make 6ch, join with sl st to first ch to form ring.

1st round 3ch to count as first dc, work 2 dc into ring, (3ch, 3dc into ring) 3 times, 3ch, join with sl st to 3rd of first 3ch.

2nd round Sl st over next 2dc and into 3ch sp, 3ch to count as first dc, work 2dc into same sp, 3ch, (1ch, 3dc, 3ch and 3dc all into corner 3ch sp) 3 times, 1ch, sl st into 3rd of first 3ch.

Work 6 more rounds, working 1 more dc group in each round between corner

groups, so having six dc groups between each corner on last round.
Fasten off.
Make 24 more squares in same way.

To finish
Placing motifs as shown in diagram, alternating one rose motif with one plain motif, join motifs as foll: with right sides tog, using size F (4.00mm) hook and B and working through double thickness work 2sc into corner sp, *working into back loops only work 1sc into each of next 3dc, 1sc into next ch sp, rep from * 6 times more, 2sc into corner sp. Do not fasten off but cont to join motifs until row of 10 motifs have been joined. Being very careful not to let motifs twist, join 4 more rows of motifs.
Join the rows of motifs together in the same way.

The border
Working along two long sides and one short end work as foll.

1st row Join B to corner sp and using size F (4.00mm) hook work 3ch to count as first dc, 2dc into same sp, * 1ch, 3dc into next space, rep from * all around 3 edges working 3dc, 3ch and 3dc all into corner ch sp.
Fasten off.

2nd row Join on C and working into 3rd ch of first 3ch of previous row work 4ch, *3dc into next 1ch sp, 1ch, rep from * all around 3 edges working 3dc, 3ch and 3dc into corner ch sp.
Fasten off.

3rd row Join on D and work as first row.
4th row Join on A and work as 2nd row.
5th row Join on A and work as first row.
Cont in stripe sequence as set, patt 23 more rows.

Top border
Work in rows along top edge, working 2 rows in A, 1 row in B, 1 row in C and 1 row in D.
Fasten off.

Lining
If you wish to line bedspread, turn in ¾in (2cm) double hem all around fabric and slip stitch in place.

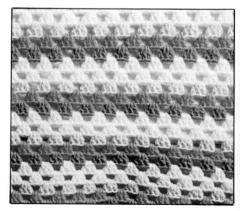

Pincushions

Two pretty and practical pin-cushions for you to make. Wear one on your wrist or hang the other around your neck, so your pins will always be close at hand.

Materials for each pincushion
7in (18cm)-diameter circle of floral print fabric
Two 4¾in (12cm) squares of felt in harmonizing colors
Matching sewing thread
Suitable stuffing; tracing paper
1yd (1m) of narrow cord for hanging pincushion or
4¾in (12cm) of ¾in (2cm)-wide elastic and strip of matching floral fabric 8×2¼in (20×6cm) for wrist pincushion

1 Run a line of gathering stitches around the floral cotton circle, ⅜in (1cm) from outer edge.
2 Draw up gathering thread and at the same time stuff the circle firmly to make a ball-like pad. Secure loose ends of gathering thread firmly at the back.
3 Trace patterns for scallop petals. Cut a set of scallop petals from each felt square.
4 Center the smaller set of scallop petals on larger set of scallop petals. Place the floral pad on top of them both with the gathering on the underside. Pin together.
5 Sew the three layers together with small neat stitches.
6 For the hanging pincushion, fold the cord in half and sew the two ends to the center of the underside of the pin-cushion so that it can be worn around the neck. Knot ends of cord to prevent raveling.
7 For the wrist pincushion, fold the floral cotton strip in half lengthwise. Pin, baste and stitch down the long sides ⅜in (1cm) from edges. Turn strap right side out.
8 Thread elastic through strap, securing one end and finishing raw edge. Gather all the fabric strap over the elastic; finish and secure the other end.
9 Stitch ends of strap to the wrong side of the pincushion, centering strap with ends 1⅛in (8cm) in from scalloped edges, so pincushion will fit over the wrist.

Kim Sayer

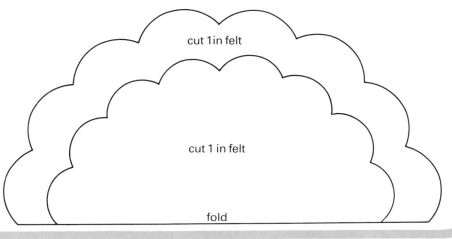

John Hutchinson

cut 1 in felt

cut 1 in felt

fold

Knitting / COURSE 24

Introducing cable patterns

Cables are among the most popular and adaptable of knitting motifs. They derive from "fisherman's knitting," such as that done in the Aran Islands off the coast of Ireland, and in some of the coastal areas of Britain, and they suggest the ropes used in fishing. Many variations of cable patterns have been devised over the years. You can use a cable singly as a panel, or combine several cables in an allover pattern. A single cable—usually worked against a purl background—is a versatile form of decoration for a plain cardigan or sweater. You can add a cable detail up the center of a sleeve or at each side of the front bands of a cardigan. Plan the style and position of the cable before you begin knitting.

Producing a cable twist involves moving a group of stitches from one position within the cable to another during the course of one row. The move is made with the help of a special, short double-pointed cable needle that holds the stitches during the transfer. There are very few sizes of cable needle; if you are unable to find the same size as the needles you are using, choose a thinner cable needle, so as not to stretch and spoil the appearance of the stitches.

The following step-by-step pictures show the basic cable techniques used in all cable patterns.

Twisting cables from right to left

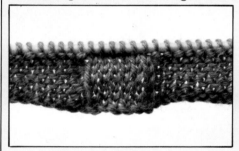

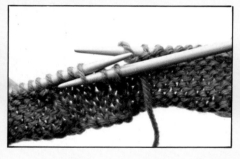

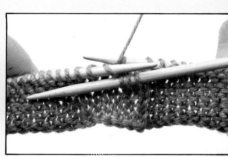

1 Cables, worked over a number of knitted stitches, show up in sharp relief against a purl background. For this sample, work six rows straight before working the cable twist. Here there are six stitches in the cable panel, but there could be any even number (four, six or eight are the most usual) depending on how wide you want the cable to be.

2 On the right side of the work, purl to the start of the cable panel. To make a twist, take the cable needle and insert it from right to left through the next stitch. Slip this stitch off the left-hand needle. Repeat for the next two stitches. Three stitches are now on the cable needle.

3 Leave the cable needle (with the stitches in the middle of it) at the front of the work, so that both left-hand and right-hand needles are behind it. Take the yarn to the back of the work and knit the next three stitches of the cable panel.

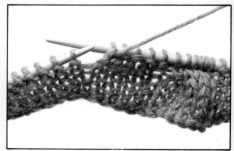

4 Now work the stitches on the cable needle. First, slide them to the right-hand end of the needle. Now you need your left hand free to guide the cable needle, and this means letting go of the left-hand needle.

5 Push the stitches down the needle to prevent them from falling off. Knit the three stitches on the cable needle from right to left.

6 The cable twist—called "cable six front (C6F)"—is now finished. It looks odd at this stage, as all the cable stitches are crowded together. Continue with the background stitches and purl to the end of the row.

7 Work seven straight rows between cable twists. Always twist the cable on the right side of the work by repeating steps 2 to 6. Here you can see the finished effect of cable twists worked from right to left on every 8th row.

8 You can vary the number of rows between twists to produce a "rope" with tighter or looser twists. This picture shows the difference between C6F worked on every 6th row—on the right—and every 10th row—on the left.

9 This photograph shows the varied effects produced if you work the cable over four stitches—on the right—and eight stitches—on the left.

Twisting cables from left to right

1 Work the first 2 steps as given for twisting cables from right to left. Leave the cable needle (with the stitches in the middle of it) at *back* of work so that both left-hand and right-hand needles are in front of it. Take the yarn to the back of the work and knit the next three stitches on the left-hand needle.

2 Now work the stitches on the cable needle; slide them to the right-hand end of the needle. Knit the three stitches on the cable needle from right to left in their correct order. See steps 4 and 5 of "Twisting cables from right to left" for hints on doing this. The cable twist is called "cable six back (C6B)."

3 In this picture there are seven straight rows between cable twists. The rope effect is similar to that made by twisting cables from right to left, only in this case the "strands" twist in the opposite direction.

Alternating cable twists

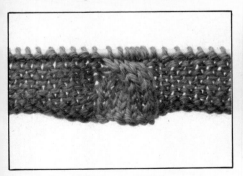

1 Work the first 6 steps as given for "Twisting cables from right to left" to produce a cable six front (C6F).

2 Work seven rows straight. On the next row twist the cable in the opposite direction—called C6B.

3 Continue to alternate the direction of the cable twists to produce a "rope" with a completely different look. Here one of the "strands" winds continuously on top of the section below.

Paul Williams

Stitch Wise

Braided cable
This cable is worked over 9 sts.
1st row (RS) K9.
2nd row P9.
3rd row Sl next 3 sts onto cable needle and leave at back of work, K3, then K 3 sts from cable needle—called C6B, K3.
4th row P9.
5th and 6th rows As first and 2nd.
7th row K3, sl next 3 sts onto cable needle and leave at front of work, K3, then K the 3 sts from cable needle—called C6F.
8th row P9.
These 8 rows form the pattern.

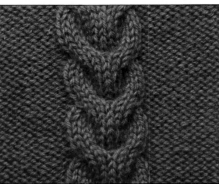

Horseshoe cable
This cable is worked over 12 sts.
1st row (RS) K12.
2nd row P12.
3rd and 4th rows As first and 2nd.
5th row Sl next 3 sts onto cable needle and leave at back of work, K3, then K the 3 sts from cable needle—called C6B—, sl next 3 sts onto cable needle and leave at front of work, K3, then K the 3 sts from cable needle—called C6F.
6th row P12.
7th and 8th rows As first and 2nd.
These 8 rows form the pattern.

Cable panel pattern
Cast on a multiple of 10sts plus 1 extra.
1st row (RS) P1, *K4, P1, rep from * to end.
2nd row K1, *P4, K1, rep from * to end.
3rd row P1, *K4, P1, sl next 2 sts onto cable needle and leave at front of work, K next 2 sts, then K the 2 sts from the cable needle—called C4F—, P1, rep from * to end.
4th row As 2nd.
5th and 6th rows As first and 2nd.
7th row P1, *C4F, P1, K4, P1, rep from * to end.
8th row As 2nd.
These 8 rows form the pattern.

Honeycomb pattern
Cast on a multiple of 8 sts.
1st row (RS) * Sl 2 sts onto cable needle and leave at back of work, K2 sts, then K the 2 sts from the cable needle—called C4B—sl next 2 sts onto cable needle and leave at front of work, K2 sts, then K the 2 sts from cable needle—called C4F, rep from * to end.
2nd row P to end.
3rd row K to end.
4th row P to end.
5th row *C4F, C4B, rep from * to end.
6th row P to end.
7th and 8th rows As 3rd and 4th.
These 8 rows form the pattern.

Cable fashion

This smart jacket trimmed with cables has its own matching hat and scarf—perfect for a trip to the zoo.

Sizes
Jacket to fit 26 [28:30]in (66[71:76]cm) chest.
Length, 16½[18:19¾]in (42[46:50]cm).
Sleeve seam, 15[15¾:16½]in (38[40:42]cm).
Hat to fit average size head.
Scarf 8in (20cm) by 35½in (90cm), excluding fringe.

Note Directions for larger sizes are in brackets []; where there is only one set of figures it applies to all sizes.

Materials

Bulky weight yarn: jacket
11[13:15]oz (300[350:400]g);
hat *4oz (100g);* scarf *6oz (150g)*
1 pair each Nos. 7 and 9 (5 and
6mm) needles
1 cable needle (called cn)
No. 7 (5mm) circular needle 40in
(100cm) long
5 buttons for jacket

Gauge

15sts and 20 rows to 4in (10cm) in stockinette st on No. 9 (6mm) needles.

Jacket

Back

Using No. 7 (5mm) needles cast on 54[58:62] sts.
1st ribbing row P2, *K2, P2, rep from *.
2nd ribbing row K2, *P2, K2, rep from *.
Rep these 2 rows for 2¾in (7cm); end with 2nd ribbing row and inc 1[2:3] sts evenly on last row. 55[60:65] sts. Change to No. 9 (6mm) needles. Beg patt.
1st row K10[11:12], P2, K6, P2, K15[18:21]. P2, K6, P2, K10[11:12].
2nd row P10[11:12], K2, P6, K2, P15[18:21], K2, P6, K2, P10[11:12].
3rd and 4th rows Rep 1st and 2nd rows.
5th row K10[11:12], P2, sl next 3 sts onto cn and leave at back of work, K3, then K sts from cn—called "cable 6 back" or

C6B; P2, K15[18:21], P2, sl next 3 sts onto cn and leave at front of work, K3, then K sts from cn—called "cable 6 front" or C6F; P2, K10[11:12].
6th row As 2nd row.
7th and 8th rows Rep 1st and 2nd rows. These 8 rows form patt. Cont in patt until work measures 11[11¾:12½]in (28[30:32]cm) from beg; end with WS row.

Shape raglan armholes

Keeping patt correct, bind off 2 sts at beg of next 2 rows.
**Next row K1, sl 1, K1, psso, patt to last 3 sts, K2 tog, K1.
Work 3 rows.
Rep last 4 rows 4[5:6] times more, then work first of these 4 rows again. Work 1 row. **. 39[42:45] sts.
Next row Bind off 13[14:15] sts, K to last 13[14:15] sts, bind off rem sts. Leave center 13[14:15] sts on holder.

Left front

Using No. 7 (5mm) needles cast on 25[29:33] sts.
1st ribbing row *P2, K2, rep from * to last st, P1.
2nd ribbing row K1, *P2, K2, rep from *.
Rep these 2 rows for 2¾in (7cm); end with 2nd ribbing row and inc 2[1:0] sts on last row. 27[30:33] sts. Change to No. 9 (6mm) needles. Beg patt.
1st row K10[11:12], P2, K6, P2, K7[9:11].
2nd row P7[9:11], K2, P6, K2, P10[11:12].
3rd and 4th rows As 1st and 2nd rows.

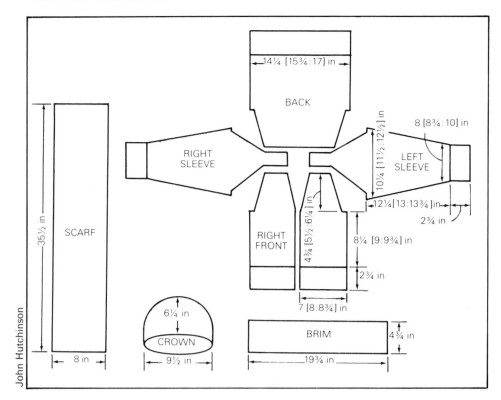

John Hutchinson

SCARF — 35½ in, 8 in

BACK — 14¼ [15¾:17] in

RIGHT SLEEVE

LEFT SLEEVE — 8 [8¾:10] in, 10¼ [11½:12½] in, 12¼[13:13¾]in, 2¾ in

RIGHT FRONT — 4¾ [5½:6¼] in, 8¼ [9:9¾] in, 2¾ in, 7 [8:8¾] in

CROWN — 6¼ in, 9½ in

BRIM — 19¾ in, 4¾ in

5th row K10[11. 12], P2, C6B, P2, K7[9:11].
6th row As 2nd row.
7th and 8th rows Rep 1st and 2nd rows. These 8 rows form patt. Cont in patt until work measures 11[11¾:12½]in (28[30:32]cm) from beg; end with WS row.
Shape raglan armhole and front edge
Bind off 2 sts at beg of next row.
Next row Patt to end.
Rep from ** to ** of back. 13[14:15] sts. Bind off.

Right front
Using No. 7 (5mm) needles cast on 25[29:33] sts.
1st row P1, *K2, P2, rep from * to end.
2nd row *K2, P2, rep from * to last st, K1. Rep these 2 rows for 2¾in (7cm); end with 2nd ribbing row and inc 2[1:0] sts on last row. 27[30:33] sts. Change to No. 9 (6mm) needles. Beg patt.
1st row K7[9:11], P2, K6, P2, K10[11:12].
2nd row P10[11:12], K2, P6, K2, P7[9:11]. Cont in patt as set, work to match left front but work C6F instead of C6B and reverse all shaping.

Left sleeve
Using No. 7 (5mm) needles cast on 30[34:38] sts and work 2 ribbing rows of back for 2¾in (7cm); end with 2nd ribbing row. Change to No. 9 (6mm) needles. Beg patt.
1st row K10[12:14], P2, K6, P2, K10[12:14].
Cont in patt as set, working C6B and inc one st at each end of 9th and every

foll 10th row until there are 40[44:48] sts. Cont without shaping until sleeve measures 15[15¾:16½]in (38[40:42]cm) from beg; end with WS row.
Shape raglan armhole
Bind off 2 sts at beg of next 2 rows.
Next row K1, sl 1, K1, psso, patt to last 3 sts, K2 tog, K1.
Next row Patt to end.
Rep these 2 rows until 14 sts rem. Cont straight on these 14 sts until saddle shoulder extension fits along 13[14:15] sts that were bound off on back and fronts; end with WS row. Cut off yarn and leave sts on holder.

Right sleeve
Work as for left sleeve but work C6F instead of C6B.

Front border
Sew saddle shoulder extensions to bound off groups on back and fronts. With RS facing and using No. 7 (5mm) circular needle join on yarn and pick up and K 52[54:56] sts along right front to beg of shaping, 19[21:23] sts to shoulder, then K2 tog at each back seam and inc one st at center of back neck on first size and dec one st at center on 3rd size, K right sleeve, back neck and left sleeve sts from holders, then pick up and K 19[21:23] sts along left front to beg of shaping and 52[54:56] sts to lower edge. 182[190:198] sts.
Next row K4, (P2, K2) to last 2 sts, K2.
Next row K2, (P2, K2) to end. Rib 1 more row.
1st buttonhole row K2, (bind off 2, rib until there are 10 sts on right-hand

needle after bound-off group) 4 times, bind off 2, rib to end.
2nd buttonhole row Rib to end, casting on 2 sts over those bound off on previous row. Rib 3 rows. Bind off in ribbing.

To finish
Press as instructed on ball band. Join raglan seams, then join side and sleeve seams. Press seams. Sew on buttons.

Hat
Main part
Using No. 9 (6mm) needles cast on 73 sts. Work in stockinette st for 3½in (9cm); end with P row.
Shape top
1st row *K7, K2 tog, rep from * to last st, K1.
2nd row P to end.
3rd row *K6, K2 tog, rep from * to last st, K1.
Cont to dec in this way, working one st less between each dec, on every other row until 17 sts rem; end with P row.
Next row (K2tog) to last st, K1.
Cut off yarn, thread through rem sts, gather tightly and secure.

Brim
Using No. 9 (6mm) needles cast on 18 sts.
1st row K2, P5, K6, P5.
2nd row K5, P6, K7.
3rd and 4th rows Rep 1st and 2nd rows.
5th row K2, P5, C6B, P5.
6th row As 2nd row.
7th and 8th rows Rep 1st and 2nd rows. These 8 rows form patt. Cont in patt until work measures approx. 20in (50cm) from beg.
Bind off.

To finish
Press as instructed on ball band. Join back seam of main part. Join cast-on and bound-off edges of brim. Sew P edge to main part so that brim turns up to right side and garter st edge turns in at top. Press seams.

Scarf
Using No. 9 (6mm) needles cast on 31 sts.
1st row K2, P4, K6, P7, K6, P4, K2.
2nd row K6, P6, K7, P6, K6.
3rd and 4th rows Rep 1st and 2nd rows.
5th row K2, P4, C6B, P7, C6F, P4, K2.
6th row As 2nd row.
7th and 8th rows Rep 1st and 2nd rows. These 8 rows form patt. Cont in patt until work measures 35½in (90cm) from beg; end with 8th row. Bind off.

Fringe
Using two 12½in (32cm) lengths of yarn tog, knot fringe into every other st along each short end. Trim ends.

Knitting / COURSE 25

Bobble stitches

The raised stitches of a bobble make an unusual and highly textured fabric. Bobble stitches are often used in Aran knitting to symbolize a rock or boulder in a seascape. They can form an allover pattern, such as trinity stitch, or, spaced out, can be combined with cables in beautiful designs.

There are various ways of making a bobble; all are based on the principle of creating a number of stitches out of one. Here we describe two methods. One of the methods involves working the bobble stitches over several rows—while working the main fabric—and then decreasing to a single stitch.

Alternatively, you can work the bobble stitches separately from the main fabric; in this case you work several rows on the bobble stitches only and reduce them to the original one before carrying on with the background.

Basic method of making a bobble

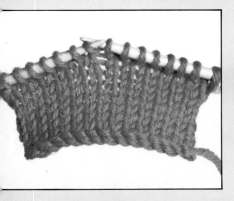

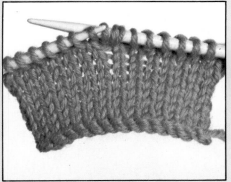

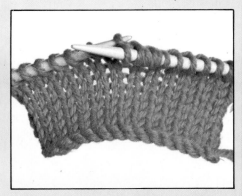

1 This technique makes a reverse stockinette stitch bobble, worked over a number of rows, against a background of the same fabric. First, work to the position of the bobble on a WS (knit) row. Knit the next stitch in the usual way, but without dropping the loop from the left-hand needle.

2 Bring the yarn forward and purl the loop on the left-hand needle: take the yarn to the back again and knit the loop. There are now three loops on the right-hand needle.

3 Purl and knit again—still keeping the loop on the left-hand needle—to make five loops on the right-hand needle. Allow the original loop to drop from the left-hand needle.

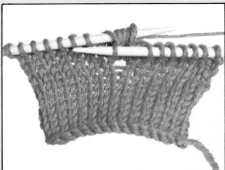

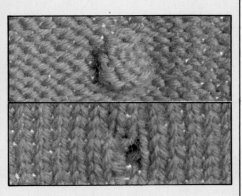

4 Continue to the end of the row, then work three rows in reverse stockinette stitch, ending with a P row. At this point the increased stitches form a slight bump on the right side of the work.

5 On the following (knit) row, work to the position of the five bobble stitches and reduce them to their original stitch by knitting them all together. Knit to the end of the row, then continue in reverse stockinette stitch.

6 The bobble formed resembles a large "blister" on the right side of the fabric. Using this method you can position bobbles at random or make an allover fabric. On the wrong side the bobble makes a dent in the fabric.

Fred Mancini

Alternative method of making a bobble

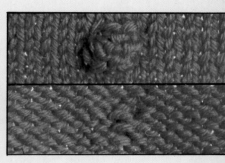

1 This technique makes a reverse stockinette stitch bobble, based on a single stitch, against a stockinette stitch background. On a knit row, make five stitches out of one (see steps 1, 2 and 3 of basic method, page 39). Turn and knit these stitches: turn and purl them.

2 Five bobble stitches are now on right-hand needle. Use left-hand needle point to lift second bobble stitch over first and off right-hand needle; repeat this process with third, fourth and fifth stitches until a single bobble stitch remains.

3 A small, neat bobble resembling those in Popcorn stitch (see Stitch Wise) is formed on the right side of the fabric. The only sign of the bobble on the back of the fabric is a slight irregularity in the knitting at the position of the bobble.

Cluster stitches

Cluster stitches are very similar to—and often confused with—bobble stitches. The basic method of working clusters is the same as for bobbles: increasing a number of stitches out of one, then either working the cluster in one with the background or finishing it separately.

Generally cluster patterns are larger than those for bobbles: the shaping is much more gradual than for a bobble and so requires more rows of knitting. Becaus? of their size, some cluster patterns ar? often used quite separately on a fabric. They are also ideal for border patterns like the one used on the woman's jacket page 42.

Basic method of making a cluster

1 Make a detached cluster in reverse stockinette st against a stockinette st background. Work to cluster position on purl row; keep yarn at front and knit next stitch to increase one stitch.

2 Don't drop the original stitch from the left-hand needle. Bring the yarn forward again and knit the original stitch.

3 Repeat the last sequence to make six loops on the right-hand needle out of one stitch. Allow the original stitch to drop from the left-hand needle.

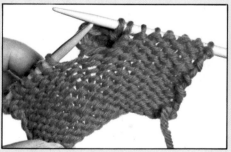

4 Turn the work so that right side is facing. Always slipping first stitch and beginning with a purl row, work four rows in reverse stockinette stitch on the six cluster stitches.

5 Turn and purl two stitches together three times across next right-side row. On the following row, slip one, knit two stitches together, then pass the slipped stitch over; one cluster stitch remains.

6 The finished cluster is attached to the main fabric by a single stitch at the start and finish; the back of the fabric is slightly marked by an irregular stitch at the position of the cluster.

Alternative method of making a cluster

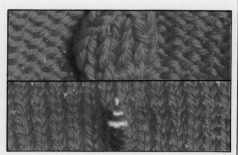

1 This technique makes a stockinette stitch cluster worked over a number of rows against a reverse stockinette stitch background. On a purl row make five stitches out of one as described in steps 1, 2 and 3 of basic method of making a bobble, page 39; work to the end of the row. Now work three more rows, reversing the background pattern over the five cluster stitches.

2 Decrease over the next three rows to shape the cluster and reduce the five stitches to one. On the next row (right side) slip the first cluster stitch, knit one, then pass the slipped stitch over; knit the next stitch, then knit the last two stitches together. Purl the three cluster stitches on the following row. Finally, on the third row (RS), slip the first stitch, knit the two stitches together and pass the slipped stitch over.

3 Although this cluster is worked flat over a number of rows, it is quite distinct against the background. The cluster covers the same area on the wrong side of the work, but it looks smaller, as the reverse side of the stitches recedes into the background.

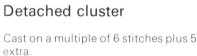

Stitch Wise

Trinity stitch

Cast on a multiple of 4 sts.
1st row (WS) *(K1, P1, K1) all into next st, P3 tog, rep from * to end.
2nd row P to end.
3rd row *P3 tog, (K1, P1, K1) all into next st, rep from * to end.
4th row As 2nd.
These 4 rows form the pattern.

Detached cluster

Cast on a multiple of 6 stitches plus 5 extra.
1st row (WS) P to end.
2nd row K to end.
3rd row *P5, (yo to make one st, K next st) 3 times into same st, so making 6 sts out of one, turn and P these 6 sts, turn and sl 1, K5, turn and sl 1, P5, turn and sl 1, K5, turn and (P2 tog) 3 times, turn and sl 1, K2 tog, psso — called make cluster (MC), rep from * to last 5 sts, P5.
4th row K to end.
5th row P to end.
6th row K to end.
7th row P2, *MC, P5, rep from * to last 3 sts, MC, P2.
8th row K to end.
These 8 rows form the pattern.

Popcorn stitch

Cast on a multiple of 6 sts plus 5 extra.
1st row (WS) P to end.
2nd row K2, (K1, P1, K1, P1, K1) all into next st, turn and K these 5 sts, turn and P5. Using point of left-hand needle, lift 2nd, 3rd, 4th and 5th sts over first st and off right-hand needle — called make bobble (MB) —, *K5, MB, rep from * to last 2 sts, K2.
3rd row P to end.
4th row *K5, MB, rep from * to last 5 sts, K5.
These 4 rows form the pattern.

A peal of bells

This jacket, with its decorative border of bell clusters, is long enough to replace a coat on a cool spring day. The attractive ribbed circular yoke echoes the border motif, and the outfit is completed with a matching scarf.

Matt White

Sizes

Jacket To fit 32[34:36:38]in (82[87:92:97]cm) bust.
Length, 32¾[33½:34¼:35]in (83[85:87:89]cm).
Sleeve seam, 17¼in (44cm).
Note Directions for larger sizes are in brackets []; where there is only one set of figures it applies to all sizes.

Materials

Jacket: 17[19:20:22]oz (480[520:560:600]g) of a bulky knitting yarn
Scarf: 6oz (160g)
1 pair of No. 8 (5½mm) needles
No. 8 (5½mm) circular needle
4 buttons

Gauge

13 sts and 22 rows to 4in (10cm) in stockinette st on No. 8 (5½mm) needles.

Jacket

Main part (one piece to underarm)
Using No. 8 (5½mm) circular needle cast on 116[124:132:140] sts for entire lower edge. K4 rows.
Next row K to end.
Next row K3, P to last 3 sts, K3.
Rep these 2 rows until work measures 4in (10cm) from beg; end with WS row. Beg patt.
1st row (RS) K3, P to last 3 sts, K3.
2nd row K to end.
3rd row K3, P1, *turn and cast on 8 sts, turn and P4, rep from * to last 4 sts, turn and cast on 8, turn and P1, K3.
4th row K4, *P8, K4, rep from * to end.
5th row K3, P1, *K8, P4, rep from * to

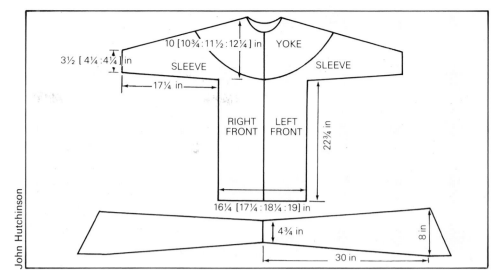

John Hutchinson

---

ast 12 sts, K8, P1, K3.
th row As 4th row.
th row K3, P1, *sl1, K1, psso, K4, K2
og, P4, rep from * to end, but finish last
ep P1, K3.
th row K4, *P6, K4, rep from * to end.
th row K3, P1, *sl 1, K1, psso, K2, K2
og, P4, rep from * to end, but finish last
ep P1, K3.
0th row K4, *P4, K4, rep from * to end.
1th row K3, P1, *sl1, K1, psso, K2 tog,
4, rep from * to end, but finish last rep
1, K3.
2th row K4, *P2, K4, rep from * to end.
3th row K3, P1, *K2 tog, P4, rep from *
o end, but finish last rep P1, K3.
4th row K4, *P1, K4, rep from * to end.
5th row K3, P1, *P2 tog, P3, rep from *
o end, but finish last rep P2 tog, K3.
6th row As 2nd row.
7th row K3, P3, *turn and cast on 8,
urn and P4, rep from * to last 6 sts, turn
nd cast on 8, turn and P3, K3.
8th row K6, *P8, K4, rep from * to end,
ut finish last rep K6.
att further 12 rows keeping "bell"
haping above cast-on sts as before.
eeping 3 sts at each end in garter st, beg
ith K row, proceed in stockinette st
ntil work measures 22¾in (58cm) from
eg; end with K row.

Divide for armholes
Next row K3, P25[27:29:31], bind off 4,
until there are 52[56:60:64] sts on
ight-hand needle after bound-off group,
ind off 4, P to last 3 sts, K3. Cont on
ast set of 28[30:32:34] sts for right
ront.
Next row K to last 3 sts, K2 tog, K1.
Next row P to last 3 sts, K3.
Rep last 2 rows 0[2:4:6] times more.
7 sts. Leave sts on holder. With RS
acing rejoin yarn to inner end of sts on
eedle and work on next 52[56:60:64]
ts for back.
Next row K1, sl1, K1, psso, K to last 3 sts,
2 tog, K1.
Next row P to end.
Rep last 2 rows 0[2:4:6] times more.
0 sts. Cut off yarn and leave sts on
older. With RS facing rejoin yarn to
nner end of sts on needle and work on
em 28[30:32:34] sts for left front.
Next row K1, sl1, K1, psso, K to end.
Next row K3, P to end.
Rep last 2 rows 0[2:4:6] times more.
7 sts. Cut off yarn and leave sts on
older.

Sleeves
Using No. 8 (5½mm) needles cast on
4[28:28:32] sts. K4 rows. Beg with
row, cont in stockinette st until work
easures 2¾in (7cm) from beg; end with
row, and inc one st at each end of last
ow. 26[30:30:34] sts.
eg patt.
st row P to end.
nd row K to end.
rd row P1, *turn and cast on 8, turn and

P4, rep from * to last st, turn and cast on
8, P1.
Cont in patt as set so omitting garter st
border at each end until 30 rows have
been completed. Beg with K row, cont in
stockinette st but inc one st at each end of
next and every foll 8th[8th:6th:6th] row
until there are 38[42:46:50] sts. Cont
straight until work measures 17¼in (44cm)
from beg; end with P row.

Shape top
Bind off 3 sts at beg of next 2 rows.
Next row K1, sl1, K1, psso, K to last 3 sts,
K2 tog, K1.
Next row P to end.
Rep last 2 rows 0[2:4:6] times more.
30 sts. Cut off yarn and leave sts on
holder.

Yoke
Using No. 8 (5½mm) circular needle and
with RS facing K sts of right front, sleeve
back, sleeve and left front; K2 tog at each
seam.
160 sts.
K1 row.
Buttonhole row K1, K2 tog, yo, K to end.
K2 rows.
Next row K3, P to last 3 sts, K3. Now
cont in ribbing as foll:
1st row K5, *P6, K2, rep from * to last 3
sts, K3.
2nd row K3, P2, *K6, P2, rep from * to
last 3 sts, K3.
3rd to 12th rows Work 1st and 2nd rows 5
times.
13th row K1, K2 tog, yo, K2, *P2, P2 tog,
P2, K2, rep from * to last 3 sts, K3. 141 sts.
14th row K3, P2, *K5, P2, rep from * to
last 3 sts, K3.
15th to 22nd rows Work in ribbing as set.
23rd row K5, *P1, P2 tog, P2, K2, rep
from * to last 3 sts, K3. 122 sts.
24th row K3, P2, *K4, P2, rep from * to
last 3 sts, K3.
25th to 28th rows Work in ribbing as set.
29th row K1, K2 tog, yo, rib to end.
30th row Work in ribbing as set.

31st row K5, *P1, P2 tog, P1, K2, rep
from * to last 3 sts, K3. 103 sts.
32nd row K3, *P2, K3, rep from * to end.
33rd to 36th rows Work in ribbing as set.
37th row K5, *P1, P2 tog, K2, rep from *
to last 3 sts, K3. 84 sts.
38th row K3, P2, *K2, P2, rep from * to
last 3 sts, K3.
39th to 42nd rows Work in ribbing as set.
43rd row K5, *P2 tog, K2, rep from * to
last 3 sts, K3. 65 sts.
K1 row.
Next row K1, K2 tog, yo, K to end. K2
rows.
Bind off knitwise.

To finish
Press with cool iron over dry cloth. Join
underarm and sleeve seams. Press seams.
Sew on buttons.

Scarf
Using No. 8 (5½mm) needles cast on 5
sts. Cont in garter st, cast on 3 sts at beg
of 3rd and every other row until there are
26 sts. K1 row.
Next row K to end.
Next row K3, P to last 3 sts, K3.
Rep last 2 rows for 2¾in (7cm); end with
WS row. Beg patt.
1st row K3, P to last 3 sts, K3.
2nd row K to end.
3rd row K3, P2, *turn and cast on 8, turn
and P4, rep from * 3 times more, turn and
cast on 8, turn, P2, K3.
Keeping edge sts and "bell" shaping as
set, cont in patt as first 16 rows of jacket.
Next row K3, P4, *turn and cast on 8,
turn and P4, rep from * to last 3 sts, K3.
Cont in patt as set, complete border.
Keeping 3 sts at each end in garter st, cont
in stockinette st, dec inside edge sts by
working K3, sl1, K1, psso, K to last 5 sts,
K2 tog, K3 on every 20th row until 16 sts
rem. Cont straight until work measures
30in (76cm) from top of garter st shaped
edge; end with WS row. Bind off. Work
2nd piece, reversing shaping. Join
bound-off edges tog. Press seam.

Toy bag

This practical toy bag is made from heavy canvas. Ribbon decorates the edges and makes the ties.

Materials

> $1\frac{3}{8}$yd (1.3m) of 36in (90cm)-wide heavy canvas
> $6\frac{1}{2}$yd (6m) of 1in (2.5cm)-wide ribbon
> Matching thread

1 To prevent shrinkage problems, wash the canvas and ribbon separately.

2 Cut a piece of canvas 28×36in (70× 90cm).

3 Turn the raw edges under $\frac{1}{4}$in (6mm) and press.

4 Lay canvas wrong side up with pressed edges upward; the selvages are the sides.

5 Pin a piece of ribbon $25\frac{1}{2}$in (90cm) long along the top so that the raw edge is covered. Stitch the ribbon in place with a heavy duty needle in your machine.

6 To make the large pocket, cut a piece of canvas measuring 18×20in (45× 50cm). Turn under a double $\frac{1}{4}$in (6mm) hem on one short edge. Pin and stitch in place.

7 Turn under 3in (7.5cm) along the other short edge of pocket and press. Then fold again, $1\frac{1}{2}$in (3cm) from first fold to make a pleat.

8 Pin the pocket to lower right-hand corner of the canvas with the raw edges even and the pleat folded flat.

9 Pin a piece of ribbon 40in (100cm) long on the right-hand side edge so that the extra $12\frac{1}{2}$in (32cm) overlaps at the top. Topstitch both edges.

10 Cut a piece of canvas measuring 18× 13in (45×33cm). Turn under double $\frac{1}{4}$in (6mm) hem on one long edge. Pin and stitch in place.

11 Repeat step 7 on the other long edge.

12 Pin this pocket to the bottom left-hand corner of the canvas with edges even and the pleat folded flat.

13 Cut a piece of canvas 7×18in (18× 45cm). Make a double $\frac{1}{4}$in (6mm) hem on one edge and a single $\frac{1}{4}$in (6mm) hem on the other.

14 Pin this pocket 5in (13cm) above the lower pocket with double hem upward. Topstitch lower edge in place.

15 Pin a piece of ribbon 40in (100cm) long along the left-hand edge and another in the center so that the extra ribbon overlaps at the top. Topstitch close to the edges.

16 Pin a piece of ribbon $35\frac{1}{2}$in (90cm) long along the bottom edge, mitering the

corners. Topstitch along both edges, without catching in pleat folds.

17 Cut the leftover ribbon into three pieces and stitch them behind the three extra lengths of ribbon along the top.

18 Topstitch upper and lower left-hand pockets as desired to make smaller pockets in them.

*Knitting in rounds with four needles
*Knitting in rounds to make stitch patterns
*Making a pompom
*Patterns for mother and daughter hats and leg warmers

Knitting in rounds with four needles

Knitting in rounds is the method used to make socks, gloves and anything else in which a seamless fabric is required. A circular needle is normally used for this purpose if the fabric is wide, but on a narrow fabric—for socks or a turtleneck, or example—the knitting is normally done with a special set of four needles which are pointed at both ends. Three of the needles hold the stitches in a triangular shape; the fourth needle is held in the right hand and used to knit the stitches. When all the stitches from one needle have been knitted, that needle becomes the working needle. As you work, the right side of the fabric is always facing you. At first it is difficult to work this way, because the needles are awkward to manage, but it becomes easier with practice.

1 Using the two-needle method, cast the total number of stitches required onto one of the four needles. Here there are 36 stitches.

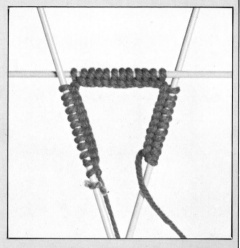

2 Divide the stitches equally between three needles—12 on each—taking great care not to twist the stitches. These three needles represent the left-hand needle in flat knitting. Tie a marker loop of yarn in a contrasting color to the left-hand end of the stitches to denote the beginning of new rounds.

3 Arrange the stitches in a triangle—they must not be twisted; ready to begin knitting; the marker loop is at the right-hand end of the third needle. Take the fourth—or right-hand—needle and slip the marker loop onto it.

4 Insert the fourth needle into the first stitch on the third needle and knit in the usual way. The triangle is now joined. Pull the yarn tightly across from the previous stitch when changing needles or there will be a loose stitch at the beginning of each needle.

5 Continue knitting each stitch from the third needle onto the fourth. When all these stitches have been knitted, the third needle is free and in turn becomes the working needle.

continued

Fred Mancini

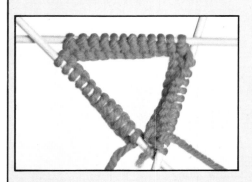

6 Continue to work in a clockwise direction, knit the stitches on the second needle until it becomes free; use this free needle to knit the stitches on the first needle. One round is now complete.

7 Remember that the right side of the fabric is always on the outside (facing) as you work a tubular fabric. To continue in stockinette stitch, slip marker loop and knit each stitch in second round. If the "purl" ridge of the wrong side of the knitting is facing out on any of the needles, the stitches are twisted.

8 Always slip the marker loop at the beginning of each round so that you don't lose your place. Continue to knit each stitch in every round until the fabric is the depth you wish. The smooth side of stockinette stitch fabric must always be on the outside. Finish at the end of a complete round (at the marker).

9 Before binding off, discard the marker loop. Knit the first two stitches of the next round onto the fourth needle: bind off by the usual method of using the left-hand (or third) needle point to lift the first stitch knitted over the second and off the fourth needle.

10 Continue binding off across the third needle until one stitch remains on the right-hand needle; use this needle holding the single stitch to bind off the stitches on the second needle and so on across the first needle until one stitch remains. Fasten off in the usual way.

11 This picture shows a continuous piece of tubular fabric without any side seams. The smooth side of the stockinette stitch fabric is on the outside. For a reverse stockinette stitch fabric, turn the work inside out.

Making a pompom

Pompoms are ornamental tufts of yarn, which make excellent trimmings for hats, berets, scarves and babies' and children's clothes. Making them is easier than you might think—in fact, children find them great fun to make. The only materials you need are the yarn, a tapestry needle and two cardboard disks. Both disks must be the same size; their diameter governs the size of the finished pompom.

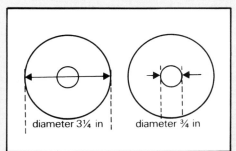

diameter 3¼ in   diameter ¾ in

1 Cut out twin cardboard rings with a diameter about 1 in (2.5cm) greater than the finished size of the pompom. The hole in the center should be one quarter the diameter of the circle.

2 Place the circles together. Thread a long piece of yarn in a tapestry needle; wind the yarn evenly around the rings, using more yarn as necessary, until the hole is full. Plenty of yarn is needed to make a good thick pompom. For a mottled effect, use two different yarns wound on at random.

Knitting in rounds to make stitch patterns

Knitting in rounds differs from flat knitting in that the right side of the work is always facing you. This produces some interesting results if you try to produce the basic stitch patterns in the normal way. By following the directions given here you will discover the special characteristics of circular knitting and learn how to form the basic fabrics that can be made, including striped patterns, by working in this way.

One advantage of working stitch patterns in rounds is that you can always keep track of the pattern as it forms on the right side. Also, there is no need for the extra edge stitches allowed for seams in flat knitting. Simply use an exact multiple of the stitches in the pattern repeat.

Garter stitch Just as the garter stitch method for flat knitting produces stockinette stitch when knitted in rounds, so the stockinette stitch method, knitted in rounds, produces garter stitch. You must knit one round and purl one round alternately to produce the characteristic horizontal ridges.

Stripes Join in a new color to the first stitch of a round. Work as many rounds as you like for each stripe. If your stripes are relatively narrow, as they are here, you can carry the strands loosely up the fabric instead of breaking off the yarn after each stripe. Notice that the stripes have a slightly staggered effect at the color change; as the knitting forms a spiral, the last stitch in the old color is next to the first stitch in the new color.

Stockinette stitch This is formed by knitting every round, as shown in detail on pages 45-46. The exterior of the tube has the familiar chain stitch effect, while the interior is ridged in the same way as reverse stockinette stitch.

Ribbing In every round you must knit each knitted stitch and purl each purled stitch. Remember that there is no selvage, so the total number of stitches must be a multiple of the number of stitches in each rib, or—if you are working a pattern with different numbers of knit and purl stitches—a multiple of each pattern repeat. Ribbing worked in rounds is a good way of making the neckband of a garment.

This photo shows the wrong side of the striped fabric, with the yarn carried up from one stripe to another. Note that you can work an uneven number of rows in a stripe and still have the yarn in the right place for picking up when you next need to knit with it.

3 Insert the scissor point between the two pieces of cardboard at the outer edge and cut the threads all around. Take care not to let the threads slip through the hole.

4 Gently separate the cardboard rings and wind a long piece of yarn (we have used a contrasting yarn for clarity) around the center, then tie it to secure the pompom. You can leave a long end to use for attaching the pompom later.
Ease the cardboard disks over the strands at each side of the pompom.

5 Shake the pompom gently so the strands form a sphere, concealing the yarn used for tying. Trim any protruding ends to give the pompom a smooth shape.

Fred Mancini

Plié perfect

Pair these easy-to-knit leg warmers with a matching hat for high-fashion outdoor wear with maximum comfort.

Sizes

To fit approx. 5-8 years [9-12 years: average woman's size].
Leg warmers length, 16[20:24]in (40[50:60]cm), adjustable.

Note Directions for larger sizes are in brackets []; if there is only one set of figures it applies to all sizes.

Materials

Knitting worsted yarn:
Garter st hat *1[1:2]oz (25[25:50]g) each in white, pale green, dark green, pale pink and dark pink*
Hat with ribbed brim *3[4:4]oz (75[100:100]g) in dark pink*
Seed st hat *2[3:3]oz (50[75:75]g) in dark green; 1oz (25g) each in white, pale green, pale pink and dark pink*
Striped stockinette st hat *1[1:2]oz (25[25:50]g) in pale green; 1oz (25g) each in white, dark green, pale pink and dark pink*
Four No. 5 (4mm) double-pointed needles
Leg warmers *5[6:7]oz (125[150: 175]g)*
Four Nos. 2, 3, 4 and 5 (3, 3$\frac{1}{4}$, 3$\frac{3}{4}$ and 4mm) double-pointed needles

Gauge

22 sts and 30 rows to 4in (10cm) in stockinette st on No. 5 (4mm) needles.

Garter stitch hat

Using set of No. 5 (4mm) needles and white, cast on 96[104:112] sts. Cont in rounds of garter st, working 4 rounds each in white, pale pink, dark green, pale green and dark pink throughout, for 5[5$\frac{1}{2}$:6]in (12[14:16]cm), finishing at end of a stripe. Turn work inside out to reverse for turn-up brim and cont in stripes until work measures 11[12:13$\frac{1}{2}$]in (28[31:34]cm) from beg, finishing at end of a stripe. Cut off yarn, thread through sts, gather up and fasten off.

Hat with ribbed brim

Using set of No. 5 (4mm) needles and dark pink, cast on 96[104:112] sts and work 5[5$\frac{1}{2}$:6]in (12[14:16]cm) in rounds of K2, P2, ribbing. Cont in stockinette st until work measures 11[12:13$\frac{1}{2}$]in (28[31:34]cm) from beg. Cut off yarn, thread through sts, gather up and fasten off. Make pompom and attach to top of hat.

Serge Krouglikoff

Seed stitch hat

Using set of No. 5 (4mm) needles and white, cast on 96[104:112] sts. Cont in garter st, working 2 rounds each in white, pale pink, dark green, pale green and dark pink, for 5[5½:6]in (12[14:16]cm). Cont in seed st with dark green only until work measures 11[12:13½]in (28[31: 34]cm) from beg.
Cut off yarn, thread through sts, gather up and fasten off.

Striped stockinette stitch hat

Using set of No. 5 (4mm) needles and pale green, cast on 96[104:112] sts. Cont in stockinette st, working 36[41:46] rounds in pale green, 18[19:20] rounds in pale pink, 14[15:16] rounds in dark green, 10[11:12] rounds in dark pink and 6[7:8] rounds in white. Cut off yarn, thread through sts, gather up and fasten off.

Leg warmers

Using set of No. 2 (3mm) needles cast on 56[64:72] sts. Work 3[3½:4]in (8[9:10]cm) in rounds of K2, P2 ribbing.
Change to No. 3 (3¼mm) needles and rib until work measures 7[9:10]in (18[22:25]cm). Change to No. 4 (3¾mm) needles and rib until work measures 11[14:16]in (28[35:40]cm). Change to No. 5 (4mm) needles and rib until work measures 16[20:24]in (40[50:60]cm) or length required. Bind off *loosely* in ribbing.

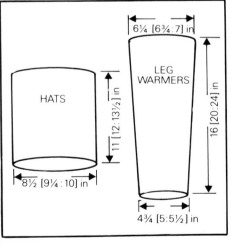

Trevor Lawrence

Tennis racquet cover

Make one of these distinctive racquet covers for every tennis player in the family using different colored ribbons and put an end to mix-ups.

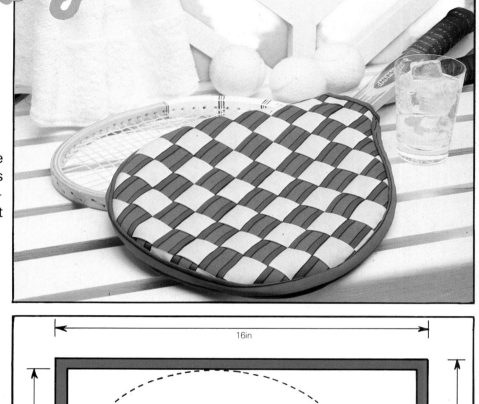

Materials

Heavy cotton fabric, 2 pieces each
12×16in (30×40cm)
Medium-weight fusible webbing
11×15in (20×38cm)
2¾yd (2.5m) of 1½in (4cm)-wide
solid-color Offray grosgrain ribbon
5¼yd (4.7m) of ⅞in (2.2cm)-wide
Offray striped ribbon
14in (35cm) of touch-and-close tape
Matching bias binding
Paper for pattern

1 Trace around the racquet on paper to make a pattern. Widen the neck by 1in (2.5cm) on each side and mark seam allowance of 1in (2.5cm) around all the edges. Cut out the pattern.
2 Trace the pattern onto the fusible webbing.
3 Place the fusible webbing, sticky side up, on the wrong side of one piece of the fabric, and pin securely in position.
4 Cut the striped ribbon into pieces as follows: Cut ribbon 1 to go vertically down the middle of the racquet shape to fit the edges of the pattern (see diagram). Pin both ends securely. Cut Ribbons 2 and 3 to fit on each side of Ribbon 1 to fit inside the edges of the pattern. Cut Ribbons 5 and 6, 7 and 8 and 9 and 10, positioning them against the edge of the closest ribbon, and pin each one securely at the top and the bottom.
5 Cut a piece of solid ribbon to cover the pattern horizontally, starting in the middle of the racquet cover.
6 Weave the ribbon under and over the striped ribbon and pin securely at each end. Cut pieces of the solid ribbon as needed to finish the weaving. Alternate the weaving on each row—over and under, then under and over.
7 When all the weaving is completed, press the ribbons carefully onto the fusible webbing, following the

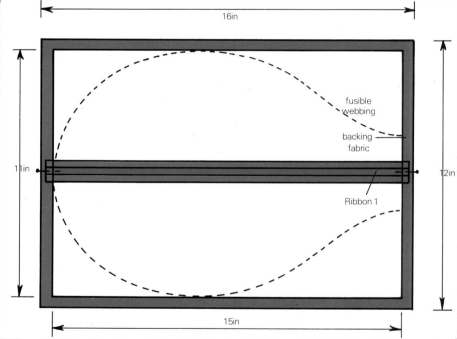

manufacturer's instructions, and carefully remove all pins.
8 Using the paper pattern, cut out the back cover from the second piece of fabric, and the front cover from the "sandwich" formed by fusing the ribbons onto the other piece of fabric.
9 Bind the curved edges of both pieces separately using the bias binding. Do NOT bind the neck edges.
10 Baste a piece of striped ribbon around the bound edge of the woven-ribbon piece, starting and finishing at the

neck edge, and stitch in place. Remove basting.
11 Join woven piece and back piece, wrong sides together, by basting and stitching the unstitched edge of the ribbon gusset to the bound edge of the back cover. Leave the cover open on the right-hand side for 14in (35cm).
12 Bind neck edge with a piece of striped ribbon.
13 Stitch touch-and-close tape in the opening or use heavy-duty snaps, spaced evenly at 1in (2.5cm) intervals.

Knitting / COURSE 27

*Choosing a circular needle
*Knitting in rounds with a circular needle to make a tubular fabric
*Increasing between stitches
*Pattern for a woman's dress

Choosing a circular needle

When you work a seamless tubular fabric, the scale of the garment—as well as the number of stitches—will determine whether you require a set of four double-pointed needles or a circular needle. Generally, circular needles are ideal for large-scale tubular knitting; you are able to work in a continuous round, without the risk of possibly stretching the stitches, as when working with four needles. You must, however, use a set of four needles for items such as seamless socks or gloves which involve fewer than about 80 stitches. Here are some points to bear in mind when you are planning to use a circular needle.

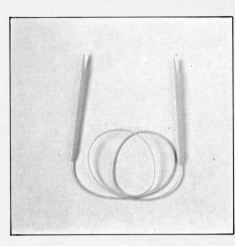

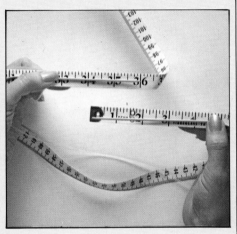

Fred Mancini

1 A circular needle usually consists of two small rigid needle-shaped sections joined by a length of flexible nylon "wire." The needle sections are available in various sizes corresponding to those of ordinary knitting needles.

2 Besides varying in diameter, circular needles also vary in length. The length is given as an overall measurement including the needles themselves and the wire; the one shown measures 36in (90cm). The needle sections are always the same length; only the length of the wire varies.

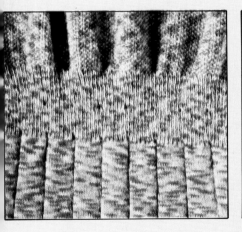

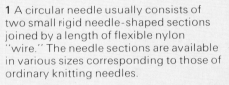

Gauge (sts to 4in)	16in	24in	Length of needle (in) 32in	36in	40in
20	80	120	160	180	200
22	88	132	176	198	220
24	96	144	192	216	240
26	104	156	208	234	260
28	112	168	224	252	280
30	120	180	240	270	300
32	128	192	256	288	320
34	136	204	272	306	340
36	144	216	288	324	360

3 The length of needle you require depends on the minimum number of stitches in the garment and your stitch gauge. First find the smallest number of stitches in the garment, or garment section, to be knitted in rounds. For example, if you are making the dress in this course, look through the directions and you will find that in the smallest size the minimum number of stitches is 256. This is where the bodice joins at the waist.

4 The chart above shows the minimum length of needle you require, according to the number of stitches, so that the stitches reach from one needle point to the other without stretching. Note that any circular needle can comfortably hold up to four times its minimum number of stitches; there is no need to change to a larger needle as the stitches increase.

5 You must also allow for stitch gauge. For the dress that follows, the gauge is 25 stitches to 4in (10cm): circle the figure "26" in the left-hand column. Follow the horizontal line of numbers to the right until you reach the last one that is less than the minimum number of stitches (256). In this case the number is 234, and the longest needle you should buy is one measuring 36in (90cm). A shorter needle would also serve the purpose.

Knitting in rounds with a circular needle to make a tubular fabric

The method of knitting in rounds with a circular needle is similar to using four double-pointed needles: the outside of the fabric is always facing you and all the rules regarding the formation of stitch patterns (as described on page 47) are the same. The advantage of a circular needle is that it is much more manageable and easier to hold than a set of needles. With only two needle points, instead of eight, there's no risk of losing stitches from the ends and there are no awkward joins between needles.

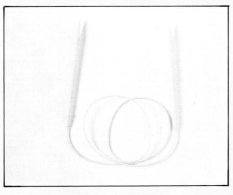

1 You may find that the length of flexible wire joining the two needle sections is twisted when you unpack the circular needle.

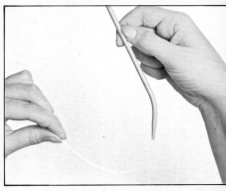

2 Straighten the twist by immersing the wire in warm water for a short time; then draw the wire between finger and thumb until it lies in a gradual curve.

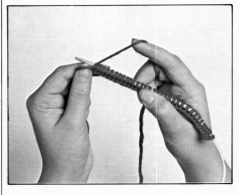

3 Cast the required number of stitches onto the section of the needle held in your right hand. When the rigid needle section is crowded with stitches, allow them to overflow onto the wire. If you cast on with one needle, a rubber band wound around the other end will prevent the stitches from slipping off.

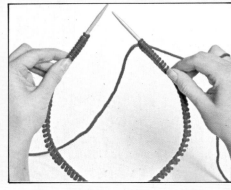

4 The total number of cast-on stitches should reach comfortably from right-hand needle point to left-hand needle point. The cast-on edge is likely to twist around the needle; to eliminate this, begin by working three rows in the normal way, as instructed in steps 5 and 6.

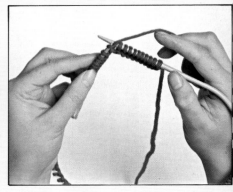

5 To work in rows, transfer the right-hand needle to the left hand and vice versa so that the first stitch, with the yarn ready to knit it, is in the left hand. Knit each of the cast-on stitches.

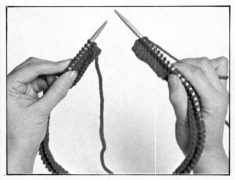

6 To work subsequent rows of a stockinette stitch fabric, transfer the needle points to opposite hands so that the first stitch to be worked is always in your left hand (as in normal knitting). Purl the second row, and knit the third.

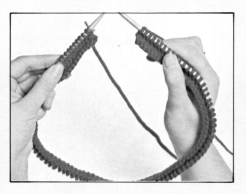

7 The ball of yarn is now at the right-hand needle section. Before joining work and knitting in rounds tie a marker loop of contrasting-colored yarn to left-hand needle section. The marker is always slipped from one needle point to the other at the beginning of a round to prevent you from losing your place.

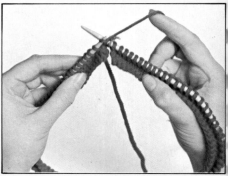

8 As you begin the first round the yarn is already attached to the stitch at the end of the right-hand needle and the right side of the fabric is facing outward. Slip marker loop onto right-hand needle, then knit first stitch on left-hand needle; pull yarn across quite tightly to avoid making a loose stitch at this join.

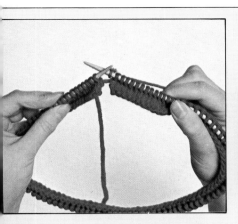

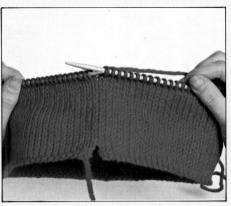

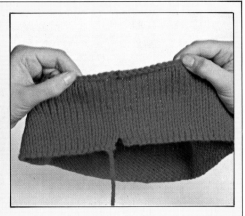

9 You have come to the end of the first round when you reach the marker loop on the left-hand needle; slip the marker before beginning the second round. At this point there is only a single horizontal strand across the join of the rounds.

10 Continue to work around in a circle; remember to knit each stitch in every round to form a stockinette stitch fabric. (For methods of working other stitch patterns in rounds see page 47.)

11 Bind off at the start of a new round. First, discard the marker loop, then knit the first two stitches of the next round, bind off the first, and continue to bind off in the usual way to the end of the round. The finished fabric is tubular except for the slit at the first three row ends; these may be seamed together.

Increasing between stitches

This is known as "making a stitch" and has the abbreviation "M1." The instructions here are for making a stitch on either a knit row or a purl row.

The method described here involves picking up the loop between two stitches and using this to form a new stitch. This method of shaping is often used in tailored garments; the resulting increase is virtually invisible.

1 Work to the position of the increase. Insert the left-hand needle from front to back under the horizontal strand of yarn lying between the next stitch on the left-hand needle and the one just knitted on the right-hand needle.

2 At this stage the picked-up loop makes a hole in the fabric. Knit the extra loop through the back to close the hole.

3 Several rows later the increase is practically invisible, except that a new stitch appears to have emerged from between the existing stitches.

4 On a purl row work to the position of the increase. Pick up a loop on the left-hand needle by inserting it from front to back under the horizontal strand of yarn lying between the two needles.

5 Now you must purl this loop through the back. Take care to insert the right-hand needle from left to right through the back loop.

Fred Mancini

Knit yourself the well dressed look

This elegant dress will see you through the afternoon and on to an evening in town. It's knitted in a variegated yarn, which is particularly effective on the bodice, knitted in seed stitch.

Sizes

To fit 32[34:36:38]in (83[87:92:97]cm) bust.
Length, 45[45½:46:46¼]in (115[116:117:118]cm) adjustable.

Note Directions for larger sizes are in brackets []; where there is only one set of figures it applies to all sizes.

Materials

18[20:20:22]oz (500[550:550:600]g) of a variegated sport yarn
1 pair each Nos. 2 and 3 (2¾ and 3¼mm) knitting needles
Nos. 0, 1, 2 and 3 (2¼, 2½, 2¾ and 3¼mm) circular needles

Gauge

23 sts and 36 rows to 4in (10cm) in seed st on No. 3 (3¼mm) needles.

Back bodice

Using No. 3 (3¼mm) needles cast on 126[140:154:168] sts for neckline and work downward. Work 1½in (4cm) K1, P1 ribbing. Beg seed st patt.
1st row *K1, P1, rep from * to end.
2nd row *P1, K1, rep from * to end. Cont in patt until work measures 15¼[15¾:16¼:16½]in (39[40:41:42]cm) from beg. Cut off yarn and leave sts on spare needle.

Front bodice

Work as for back bodice, but do not cut off yarn.

Skirt

Join front and back bodice: using No. 0 (2¼mm) circular needle work in ribbing across sts of front bodice, then across sts of back bodice. 252[280:308:336] sts. Work 2in (5cm) in rounds of K1, P1 ribbing.
Next round (eyelet-hole round) * (K1, P1) 6 times, yo, K2 tog, rep from * to end. Rib 2in (5cm) more. Change to No. 1 (2½mm) circular needle. Beg wide ribbing.
1st round *K12, P2, rep from * to end. Rep last round for 5½in (14cm). Change to No. 2 (2¾mm) circular needle. Rib 5½in (14cm). Change to No. 3 (3¼mm) circular needle. Rib a further 5½in (14cm).
Next round *K6, pick up loop lying between needles and K tbl—called make one, or M1—, K6, P2, rep from * to end. 18[20:22:24] sts increased.
Next round *K13, P2, rep from * to end. Rep last round for 5½in (14cm).
Next round *K6, M1, K7, P2, rep from * to end. 18[20:22:24] sts increased.
Next round *K14, P2, rep from * to end. Rep last round for 5in (13cm) or until dress is ¾in (2cm) less than required length. Work 6 rounds seed st, dec one st on first round. Bind off.

Armhole borders

Join shoulder seams for approx 6¼in (16cm) from each side edge. Using No. 2 (2¾mm) needles and with RS facing, beg 10in (25cm) down side seam and pick up and K 128 sts around armhole. Work 1½in (4cm) K1, P1 ribbing. Bind off in ribbing.

To finish

Join underarm seams. Press lightly as directed on ball band. Make twisted cord approx 71in (180cm) long and thread through eyelet holes at waist.

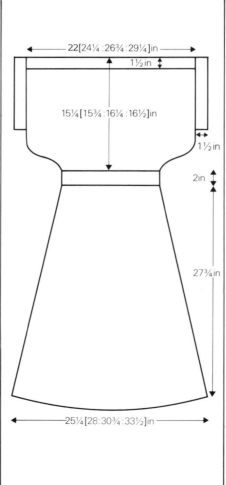

Brian Mayor

Knitting / COURSE 28

Working a chevron-striped fabric

The zigzag pattern of chevrons is formed by alternately increasing and decreasing stitches at intervals across the right-side rows throughout the fabric. Some patterns emphasize the upward and downward points of the chevrons with decorative vertical lines of shaping.

Another way of heightening the effect of a chevron fabric is to use different colors to make stripes. The various colors are added in the same way as for simple horizontal stripes, but the finished appearance is completely different.

In our sample, stockinette stitch is used

for the basic fabric. Garter stitch and some lacy patterns—which naturally entail a mixture of increasing and decreasing—can also be adapted effectively to make chevron stripes. (See shale pattern and shale and rib pattern in Stitch Wise, page 58.)

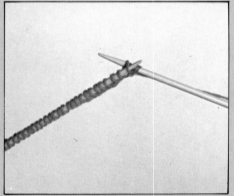

1 Cast on a multiple of 13 stitches plus 2 extra (e.g. 28, 41, 54). Work first row as follows: *knit 2, then make 1 by picking up the horizontal loop lying between the needles and knitting through the back of it.

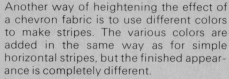

2 Complete the first row: knit 4, slip 1 purlwise, knit 2 together, pass slipped stitch over, then make 1 as in step 1. Repeat this sequence from * to last 2 stitches; knit 2.

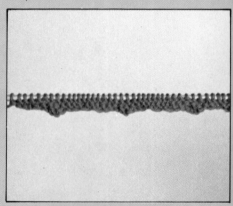

3 On the 2nd row and all following wrong-side rows—simply purl every stitch to the end of the row.

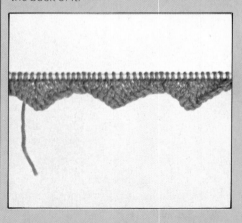

4 The 1st and 2nd rows are repeated throughout to create the chevron fabric. Work two more rows before joining in the next color.

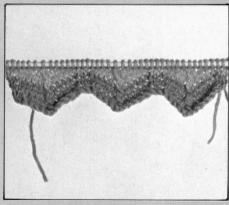

5 At the beginning of the next row join in the new color in the same way as for working horizontal stripes (Volume 3, page 26). Work four rows in pattern with the new color.

6 Continue working in four-row stripes carrying the colors not in use up the side of the work. You can vary the number of rows in each stripe as long as it is an even number. You must always change colors on a right-side row so that the color change does not show.

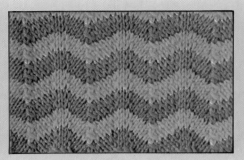

7 Bind off when you reach the length you require. Note the distinctive lower edge of the fabric as the chevrons dip at the points where stitches have been decreased and rise where stitches have been increased.

8 To make deeper chevron points, work fewer stitches between the shaping position. To do this you must cast on a different number of stitches. For example, cast on multiples of 11 stitches instead of 13, and knit 3 stitches instead of 4 between shaping.

9 Chevron points can be made shallower by increasing the number of stitches between shaping points. Here multiples of 17 stitches have been cast on and 6 stitches (instead of 4) separate the shaping positions.

Working a herringbone casing over elastic

The most popular kind of skirt waist-band is a piece of elastic placed just inside the upper edge and held in place with herringbone stitches. The elastic should be specially made for waistbands —flat and at least 1 in (2.5cm) wide. Cut it to fit your waist measurement—not the finished waistband.
After the herringbone stitching is complete, the elastic should move freely within the casing and not be caught down.

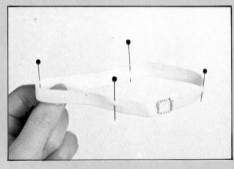

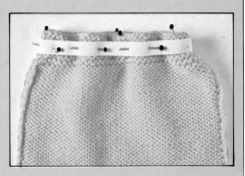

1 Cut the elastic to your waist measurement plus an extra $1\frac{1}{4}$in (3cm). Overlap the ends for $\frac{5}{8}$in (1.5cm) to make a circle. Secure ends by overcasting. Mark circle into four equal quarters with pins.

2 Join the skirt sections. Divide the upper edge into quarters marking the four points with pins. On the wrong side of the waistband pin the elastic in place matching the quarter-section pins on elastic and skirt. You may need to stretch the elastic slightly to fit. Remove quarter pins before sewing.

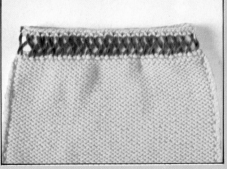

3 Thread a blunt-ended yarn needle with matching yarn (here it is in a contrasting color for clarity); anchor yarn to left-hand side seam. Hold the waistband and slightly stretched elastic over the fingers of your left hand. Insert the needle from right to left through two stitches at the top of the elastic.

4 Work the herringbone stitches from left to right. Take the yarn diagonally down across the elastic to the lower edge and insert the needle from the right to left through the next two stitches to the right. Make another stitch above the elastic, diagonally to the right, catching the next two stitches at the top of the elastic.

5 Continue this way, alternating stitching on each side of elastic until it is secured all around waistband. Distribute the knitting evenly and do not catch the elastic in the stitching.

Fred Mancini

Stitch Wise

Shale pattern

Two colors are required for this pattern. Using the first color, cast on a multiple of 11 sts.

1st row (RS) *(K2 tog) twice, (yo, K1) 3 times, yo, K2 tog, K2 tog, rep from * to end.
2nd row P to end.
3rd row K to end.
4th row K to end.
Join in the second color and repeat the 4 patt rows in stripes throughout.

Shale and rib pattern

Five toning colors are required for this pattern. Using the first dark color, cast on a multiple of 17 sts plus 2 extra.

1st row (RS) *K2, P2, K2 tog tbl, (K1, yo) 6 times, K1, K2 tog, P2, rep from * to last 2 sts, K2.
2nd row P2, *K2, P15, K2, P2, rep from * to end.
3rd row *K2, P2, K3 tog tbl, K9, K3 tog, P2, rep from * to last 2 sts, K2.
4th row P2, *K2, P11, K2, P2, rep from * to end.
Work from dark to light colors. Join in the second color and repeat the 4 patt rows in stripes throughout, then repeat the sequence with the remaining 3 colors.

Note When changing colors you must knit the stitches in the first row that you previously purled in order to keep unbroken lines of color on the right side of the work.

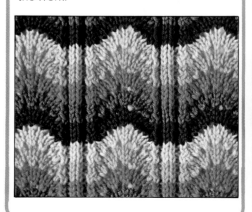

Shapely chevrons

Chevrons are flattering to any figure. Make this gently flared skirt in harmonizing shades, and pair it with a dashing chevron-striped scarf.

Sizes
Skirt to fit 34[36:38]in (86[91:97]cm) hips.
Length, 29½in (75cm).
Scarf 7½in (18cm) by 59in (147.5cm), excluding fringe.

Note Directions for larger sizes are in brackets []; where there is only one set of figures it applies to all sizes.

Materials
Skirt: *Fingering yarn: 6[7:7]oz (150[175:200]g) in main color (A)*
2oz (50g) of contrasting color (B)
4[4:5]oz (100[100:125]g) of contrasting color (C)
5[6:6]oz (125[150]g) of contrasting color (D)
1 pair each Nos. 2 and 3 (2¾ and 3¼mm) needles
Waist length of 1in (2.5cm) elastic
Scarf: *3oz (75g) of yarn as above in A, 1oz (25g) in B, 1oz (25g) in C and 2oz (50g) in D*
No. 3 (3¼mm) circular needle

Note The scarf is knitted in rows on a circular needle because the number of stitches to be cast on would make it impracticable to use ordinary needles. The circular needle is used as ordinary needles would be.

Gauge
30 sts and 40 rows to 4in (10cm) in patt on No. 3 (3¼mm) needles.

Skirt
Back
Using No. 2 (2¾mm) needles and A, cast on 101[101:115] sts for waist edge and work 10 rows in garter st. Change to No. 3 (3¼mm) needles. Join on B. Beg patt.
1st row (RS) Using B, K1, sl 1, K1, psso, *K5, yo, K1, yo, K5, sl 2 tog knitwise, K1, p2sso, rep from * ending with K2 tog, K1 instead of sl 2 tog, K1, p2sso.
2nd row K7, *K1 tbl, K1, K1 tbl, K11, rep from * ending with K7.
Rep these 2 rows throughout in stripe patt of 2 rows A, 4 rows C, 2 rows A, 6 rows D, 2 rows A, 2 rows B. Work 10 rows in patt,

Kim Sayer

SCARF

7½in

59in

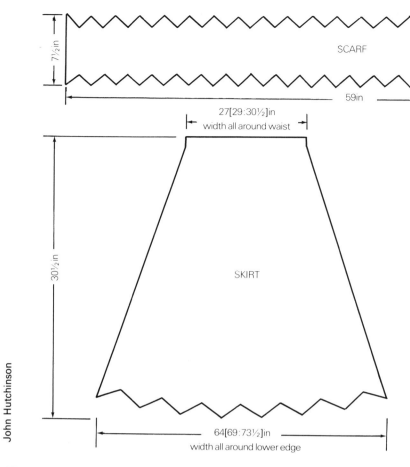

27[29:30½]in
width all around waist

30½in

SKIRT

John Hutchinson

64[69:73½]in
width all around lower edge

Shape skirt
Next row K8, *yo, K1, yo, K13, rep from * ending with K8.
Next row K to end, knitting into back of every "yo" in previous row.
Next row K1, sl 1, K1, psso, *K6, yo, K1, yo, K6, sl 2 tog, K1, p2sso, rep from * ending as first patt row. Work 7 rows as set.
Next row K9, *yo, K1, yo, K15, rep from * ending with K9.
Cont to inc in this way on every 10th row until there are 241[241:275] sts. Cont without shaping until work measures approx 29½in (75cm) from beg, ending with 6 rows in D. Using A, work 9 rows in patt. Bind off *very loosely.*

Front
Using No. 2 (2¾mm) needles and A, cast on 101[115:115] sts and work as for back, inc to 241[275:275] sts.

To finish
Do not press. Join side seams. Work herringbone casing over elastic on WS of waistband as shown on page 57.

Scarf
Using No. 3 (3¼mm) circular needle and A, cast on 443 sts and work in rows.
1st row K1, sl 1, K1, psso, *K8, yo, K1, yo, K8, sl 2 tog, K1, p2sso, rep from * ending with K2 tog, K1.
2nd row K to end, knitting into back of every "yo" in previous row.
Rep these 2 rows throughout in stripe patt of (2 rows B, 2 rows A, 4 rows C, 2 rows A, 6 rows D, 2 rows A) 4 times, then 1 row in A. Bind off *very loosely.*
Fringe Cut 12in (30cm) pieces in each of 4 colors. For each tassel take 1 strand in each color and knot tassels into every 6th row end along short ends.

Sewing / COURSE 24

*Pocket welts
*Bagging out
*Boxy vest:
 adapting the pattern
 directions for making

Pocket welts

A pocket welt is a flap which covers the opening of a pocket or is used as a decorative feature to suggest a pocket. The vest on page 63 has welts used as decorative features only.

If the fabric is firmly woven, you may not need to interface the welt, but normally interfacing is used to give added body. On a lightweight fabric, use lawn or a lightweight non-woven interfacing, and cut the interfacing the same size as the welt pattern. On heavy fabrics, use hair canvas or heavy non-woven interfacing, and cut the interfacing only half as deep as the welt, so that it adds only a single thickness.

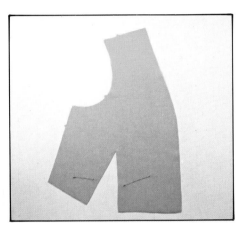

1 Mark the position of the lower edge of the welt on the front of the garment with lines of basting.

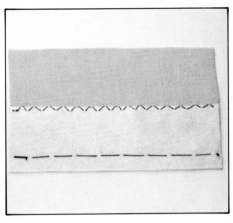

2 Cut out a piece of interfacing for each welt, to the fold line only. Baste interfacing to half of each welt on the wrong side. Catch-stitch the interfacing in place along the foldline on each welt, making sure that the stitches do not show on the right side.

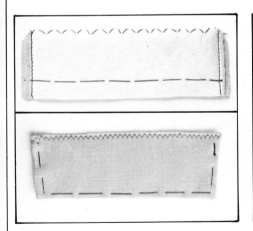

3 Fold the welt on the foldline with right sides together and stitch across the short ends.
Grade the seams, trimming away the interfacing close to the stitching, and cut off the corners.
Turn the welt right side out and baste around all four edges. Press flat. Join the raw edges together with overcasting or machine zig-zag stitches. Topstitch around the seamed edges of the welt, $\frac{1}{4}$in (6mm) from the edge.

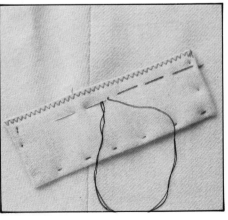

4 Baste the welt to the garment, matching the welt seamline (not the raw edge) to the basting stitches on the garment front. The folded edge of the welt must face down.
Stitch the welt in place, reversing the stitching at each end of the seam for a strong finish.

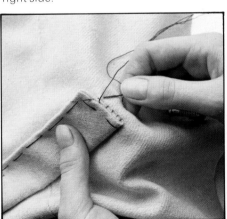

5 Press the welt upward. Slip stitch the short side edges of welt to the garment. Press.

Paul Williams

Bagging out

Bagging out is a dressmaking term for facing a garment or part of a garment completely with a lining, so that facings around the edges are unnecessary. The lining can be made from lining fabric, contrasting fabric, or even the same fabric as the garment if it is not too thick. The same pattern pieces are used for the lining as for the garment itself. When the two pieces are joined the seam encloses all the raw edges.

Patch pockets are often bagged out with lining fabric. The term "bagging out" is also sometimes used when making a collar, as all the edges are enclosed. The following steps illustrate how to bag out the vest shown on page 63.

1 Assemble the garment and lining separately, leaving the shoulder seams open. Baste them together, right sides facing, matching raw edges and seams. Stitch down the front edges, around neck and around armhole edges, to shoulder seamlines only. The bottom edge and the shoulder seams are left unstitched.

2 Remove basting and grade the seams, trimming the interfacing close to the stitching. Clip the neck and armhole curves. Turn the garment right side out, through the open hem edge. Baste around the stitched edges and press.

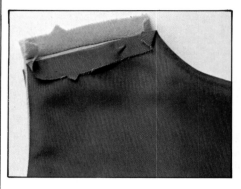

3 At the shoulder edges, fold back the seam allowances of the lining and baste and stitch the shoulder seam on the main fabric only, with right sides together and the notches matched. Press the seams open. Slip the front lining shoulder seam allowance under the back, then fold under the back seam allowance. Slip stitch the folded edge to the front lining along the shoulder line. Press.

4 Fold in the seam allowance on the bottom edge of the vest and lining and baste the two folded edges together. Press flat. Slip stitch the two edges together to complete the bagging out.

5 Topstitch the outer edges of the garment $\frac{1}{4}$in (6mm) from the edge to prevent lining rolling to the right side. Topstitch the armhole edges in the same way.

Boxy vest

This vest is the second variation on the Pattern Pack and is adapted from the jacket pattern. It coordinates with the skirt shown in Volume 5, page 68 and with the plaid shirt shown on page 70.

Adapting the pattern

Materials
2 sheets of tracing paper at least 24 × 16in (60 × 40cm)
Flexible curve

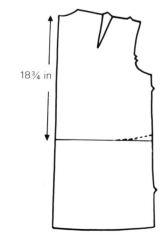

18¾ in

1 Trace the pattern pieces for the jacket back and front on the sheets of tracing paper.
Measure down the center back line 18¾in (47.5cm) from the neck edge for the length of the vest, including ⅝in (1.5cm) for a hem, and mark this point. Draw a line at right angles from the point just marked, joining the center back to the side edge. Measure ¼in (6mm) from the hem at the side edge and taper the lower edge of the vest from this point into the hemline, using a flexible curve.
If the vest needs to be shorter or longer, adjust the pattern on the alteration lines, which are marked on the pattern.

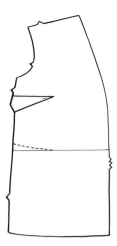

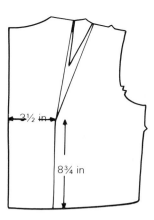

2 Mark the new side length on the front pattern piece. Do *not* include the amount taken up by the bust dart—measure down to the top of the dart, then resume measuring at its lower edge.

3½ in

8¾ in

3 A shoulder dart is not needed on the vest back, so the fullness is moved to the waist. Draw a line 3½in (9cm) away from and parallel to the center back, making it 8¾in (22.5cm) long. Draw two more lines, joining the top of this line to the points where the shoulder dart stitching lines meet the edge of the pattern.

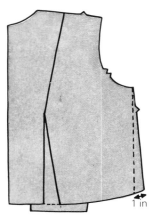

4 Cut along the lower line up to the point where the lines meet. Match the shoulder dart lines and tape them in place. This will open the waist dart. The sides of the slash form the new waist dart stitching lines. Insert paper behind the slash and draw in the lower edge of the dart.
5 Measure in 1 in (2.5cm) at lower edge of side seam and connect this point to underarm for the new cutting line.

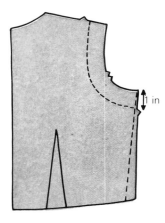

6 Measure in 1 in (2.5cm) at intervals around armhole and join points with a flexible curve for new cutting line.

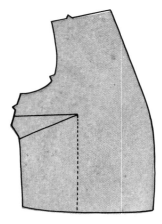

7 The bust dart fullness is put into a waist dart. Draw a line from the point of the bust dart to the lower edge of the pattern, parallel to the center front.

Terry Evans

Peter Waldman

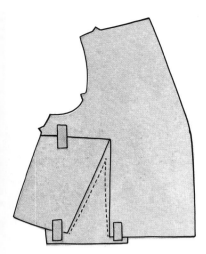

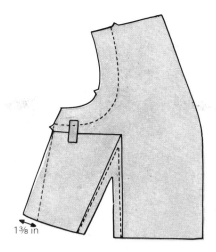

11 Mark the new armhole cutting line in the same way as for the back.

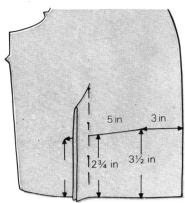

8 Cut along this line to dart point and close the bust dart, taping it in place. This opens the waist dart. Place paper under the waist dart; measure down 1in (2.5cm) from the top of the opening and mark the new dart point. Join this point to the lower sides of the slash to form the new dart stitching lines.

9 Add $\frac{5}{8}$in (1.5cm) seam allowance to the inside of both dart lines and cut away the inside of the dart on these lines. This reduces the bulk of the dart when it is stitched together.

10 Since more fitting is now needed around the lower edge, measure in 1$\frac{3}{8}$in (3.5cm) at the lower side edge of the vest and connect this point to the underarm edge to form the new cutting line. Mark in the new seamline $\frac{5}{8}$in (1.5cm) from the edge.

12 For welt position mark a point 3in (7.5cm) in from front edge and 3$\frac{1}{2}$in (9.5cm) up from lower edge. Pin waist dart and measure 2$\frac{3}{4}$in (7cm) up from lower edge on dart line. Draw a line 5in (12.5cm) long through the two points.

13 Draw a pattern for the pocket welts 6in by 3in (15.5cm by 9.5cm). Mark fold line in center of welt pattern and draw in seam lines $\frac{5}{8}$in (1.5cm) from outer edges.

Cutting layouts

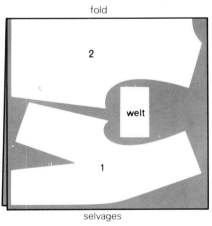

48 in & 54 in-wide fabric with or without nap
(same layout for 54 in-wide lining)

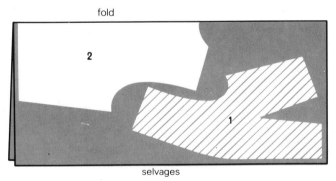

36in-wide lining

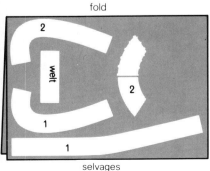

36in-wide interfacing

Key to adjusted pattern pieces

1 Vest front	Cut 2 from each fabric
2 Vest back	Cut 1 on fold from each fabric
3 Welt	Cut 2 from main fabric

Interfacing—see step 3, page 66.

Brian Mayor

65

Directions for making

Measurements

The pattern—based on the short-sleeved jacket—is given in sizes 10, 12, 14, 16, 18 and 20, $\frac{5}{8}$in (1.5cm) seam allowances are included throughout: see page 2 for a guide to size.

Suggested fabrics

Tweed, flannel, linen, synthetic suede.

Materials

48/54in (120/140cm)-wide fabric
with or without nap:
For all sizes: $\frac{3}{4}$yd (60cm)
54in (140cm)-wide lining fabric:
For all sizes: $\frac{3}{4}$yd (60cm)
36in (90cm)-wide lining fabric:
Sizes 10-12: $\frac{7}{8}$yd (80cm)
Sizes 14-20: $1\frac{1}{8}$yd (1m)
36in (90cm)-wide interfacing:
For all sizes: $\frac{5}{8}$yd (50cm)
Matching thread

1 Alter the pattern pieces for the vest front and back from the basic jacket pattern pieces (see pages 63-65).

2 Prepare the main fabric and pin on three pattern pieces following the layout given. Make sure the grain lines on the pattern are on the correct grain of the fabric. Cut out each piece, following the edges of the pattern closely. Mark the positions of the darts and welts; remove pattern pieces. Prepare the lining fabric and pin on the front and back pieces following the appropriate layout. Cut out the vest lining pieces and mark the positions of the darts.

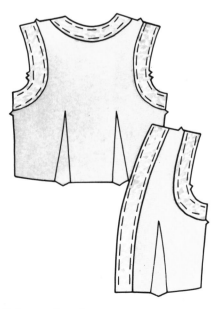

3 Cut out interfacing for the front edges, the front and back armholes and the back neck, following the outside edge of each pattern piece and making the interfacing 2in (5cm) wide.
Baste the interfacing in place on the

wrong side of the vest front and back edges. Cut out a piece of interfacing for each welt to the foldline on the pattern only.

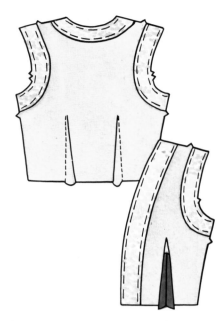

4 Fold, baste and stitch the front waist darts. Make the back waist darts in the same way.
Press the back darts toward the center back and press the front dart edges and the top of each dart flat.

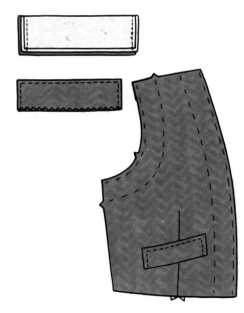

5 Interface and assemble both welts as shown on page 61.
Topstitch side and long folded edges $\frac{1}{4}$in (6mm) from the edge.
Press.
Attach the welts to the vest fronts on the positions marked, following the directions shown on page 61.

6 Baste and stitch the side seams of the vest with right sides together and notches matching. Finish the seams and press open.

7 Bag out the vest with the lining and join the shoulder seams (see page 62). Press, then topstitch around armholes, front and back edges and bottom edge, stitching exactly $\frac{1}{4}$in (6mm) in from the seam. Press.

Peter Waldman

Tool bag

Just the gift for the car enthusiast, a roll-up bag to hold all the paraphernalia needed for repairs and maintenance.

Finished size
Unrolled, the bag measures 29 × 12in (75 × 30cm) (with the flaps folded in). ¾in (2cm) seams are allowed throughout.

Materials
- 1¾yd (1.5m) of 36in (90cm)-wide heavy cotton fabric
- ⅞yd (.8m) of ⅝in (1.5cm)-wide elastic
- 1¾yd (1.5m) of ⅝ (1.5cm)-wide contrasting seam tape
- Matching thread
- Thread to match tape

1 From cotton fabric cut out two pieces each 31½ × 13½in (80 × 34cm) for bag front and back. Cut out four flap pieces, each 31½ × 6¼in (30 × 16cm).

2 On one long edge of each flap piece, trim corners into a curve.

3 Place flap pieces together in pairs. Pin, baste and stitch sides and curved long edge of each pair, leaving straight long edges open. Trim seam and turn flaps right side out. Pin and baste remaining long edges together.

4 From cotton fabric cut out two pieces each 31½ × 2¼in (80 × 6cm) for casing. Pin, baste and stitch casing pieces together to form one long strip.

5 Fold casing strip in half lengthwise with right sides together. Pin, baste and stitch down complete length. Trim and turn casing strip right side out. Press seam over center.

6 Thread elastic through casing, pinning ends of elastic to ends of casing to hold. Turn in each end of casing strip. Secure elastic firmly to each end of casing strip.

7 Center elasticized casing strip down length of front piece. Pin, baste and stitch

across casing strip at each end and at intervals down the complete length to hold tools.

8 Place flap pieces on right side of front piece at each long edge, matching raw edges. Pin in place.

9 Fold cotton tape in half lengthwise. Place folded end of tape on one short edge of front piece, corresponding to casing strip.

10 Place back piece, right side down, on front piece, enclosing flaps and tape. Pin, baste and stitch all around bag, through all thicknesses, leaving a 5in (12cm) opening in one short side. Trim seams and corners and turn right side out. Turn in opening edges and slip stitch them together.

11 Topstitch around bag using contrasting thread, about ¼in (6mm) from outer edge, and down each long side.

*Working with balanced
  plaid fabrics
*Front facing cut in one
  with a bodice
*Flat felled seam
*Coordinating shirt:
  adapting the pattern
  directions for making (1)

Working with balanced plaid fabrics

On balanced plaid fabrics the lengthwis
and crosswise stripes are arranged sym
metrically, so that the design runs th
same way both up and down and also th
same way from right to left and vic
versa. This makes it easier to work wit
than unbalanced plaids (to be discusse
in a later course); even so, extra car
must be taken when cutting out an
making a garment in this fabric.

It is inadvisable to choose a plaid fabri
for a pattern with many seams in th
bodice or skirt, as these will break th
continuity of the plaids. If a pattern ha
darts at the waistline, these can b
converted to tucks or gathers for
smoother effect. If the pattern does nc
specify the amount needed for plai
fabric, buy an extra 12-20in (30-50cm
of fabric, depending on the size of th
plaid; the larger the plaid, the mor
fabric is needed for matching the patterr

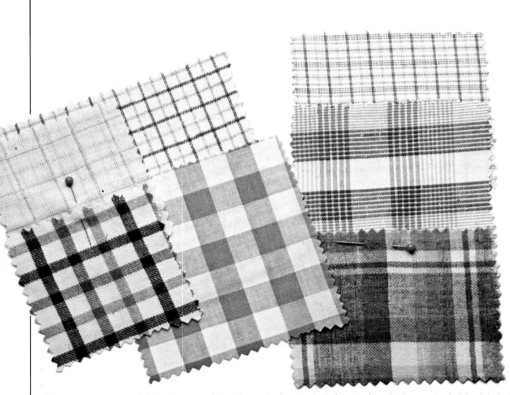

These two sets of fabric swatches show balanced (left) and unbalanced plaids (right).

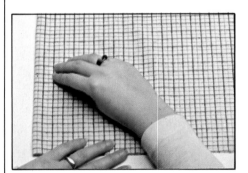

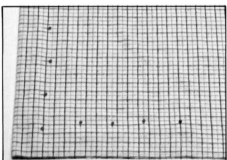

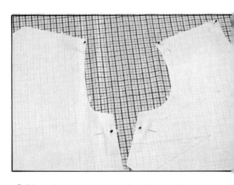

1 When preparing the fabric for cutting out, fold the fabric down the center of one plaid with right sides together. Make sure that the stripes on the two layers are lying exactly together along the whole length of the fabric. If they are not, the seams will not match when the garment is basted.

2 Pin the two layers together at the edges of the fabric to prevent them from slipping when you cut out the garment. If the plaids have been printed off the grain and the pattern does not match when the fabric is folded, cut out each pattern piece from single fabric, making sure that the plaids match.

3 Notches to be matched together must b placed on corresponding stripes. These will probably fall at the shoulder, side and waistline seams.

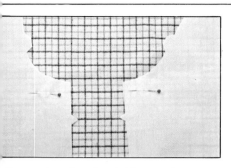

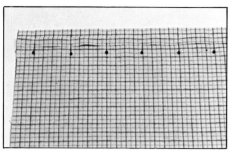

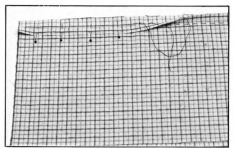

Remember that the plaids must be matched on the seamline and not the cutting line. When pinning on the sleeve pattern, make sure that the horizontal stripes will line up with those on the bodice of the garment. (With very small plaids this is not so important.)

5 The plaids must match exactly at the side seams, center seams or openings, shoulder seams, waistline, armhole and sleeves. To make sure that the plaids match exactly, slip baste the seams. To do this, first turn the seam allowance to the wrong side on one of the pieces to be joined.

6 Pin the folded edge to the seamline on the right side of the other garment piece, matching the plaids exactly. Take the basting through the fold and into the fabric exactly opposite as shown.

Front facing cut in one with a bodice

This kind of facing is often used if the edge to be finished is straight. Instead of sewing on a separate piece of fabric, you extend the main piece and fold it back to form the facing. This method is particularly well-suited to garments made of heavyweight fabrics, on which the seam allowances would be too bulky to lie smoothly.

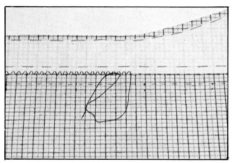

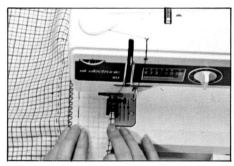

1 Transfer the markings for the foldline, center front and buttonholes to both garment front pieces. Cut out the two pieces of interfacing for the facings and baste them to the wrong side of facing with the edge to the foldline. Catch-stitch the interfacing in place along this line. Trim $\frac{1}{4}$in (6mm) from edge of interfacing.

2 Finish the outer raw edge of the facing either by turning under $\frac{1}{4}$in (6mm) of the fabric and stitching close to the edge (on lightweight fabrics) or by overcasting or zig-zag stitching the edge (on heavyweight fabrics).

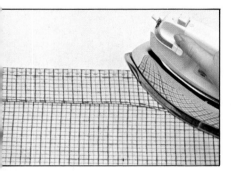

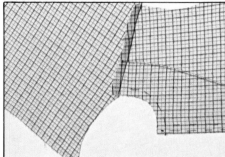

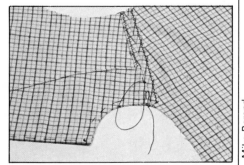

3 Fold the facing to the inside on the foldline and baste close to the edge. Press.

4 There are two methods of finishing the short upper edge of the facing if there is no back facing. Above it is stitched into the shoulder seam with the front section. The seam is then pressed flat.

5 The second method is to keep the edges of the facing free as you stitch the shoulder seam. Press the seam flat, then turn under the seam allowance on the facing and slip stitch it to the shoulder seamline. If the neck is faced at the back, join the two facings together on the shoulder seamline.

Mike Berend

Flat felled seam

This is a strong seam, for use on garments which will be subjected to a lot of heavy wear, such as men's shirts, sports wear, pajamas and children's wear. As the raw edges are all enclosed within the seam, the seam will withstand repeated washing without raveling.

The seam is most successful on thinner fabrics, on heavier material it is difficult to construct and bulky when finished. When the seam is complete, two rows of stitching will show on the right side. If you prefer, you can reverse the seam so that only one row shows on the right side. On lightweight fabrics the second row of stitches can be sewn by hand to make the seam less conspicuous.

1 Baste and stitch the seam on the seamline with wrong sides together. Press the seam open and then press both seam allowances to one side. The side to which it should be pressed will depend on the garment and will usually be specified in the pattern directions. Trim the bottom seam allowance to $\frac{1}{8}$in (3mm).

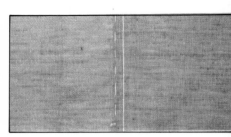

2 Fold in $\frac{1}{4}$in (6mm) of the upper seam allowance and baste it down over the trimmed edge. Stitch close to the folded edge through all thicknesses so that the raw edges are enclosed. Press flat.

Coordinating shirt

This shirt completes our three piece outfit and is adapted from the basic shirt in the Stitch by Stitch Pattern Pack. We've made it in a plaid fabric and also in a floral print. Wear it with its coordinating skirt and vest.

Adapting the pattern

Measurements
The pattern is given in sizes 10, 12, 14, 16, 18 and 20, corresponding to sizes 8 to 18 in ready-made clothes.

Materials
Sheets of tracing paper, at least 30×20in (75×50cm)
A flexible curve

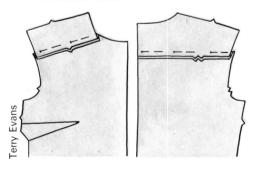

1 Pin the front yoke to the shirt front and the back yoke to the shirt back, overlapping the $\frac{5}{8}$in (1.5cm) seam allowances so that the seamlines are aligned. Trace both complete pieces—front and back—leaving an extra 6in (15cm) of paper at the front edge of the shirt. Cut out the pattern for the back.

Peter Waldman

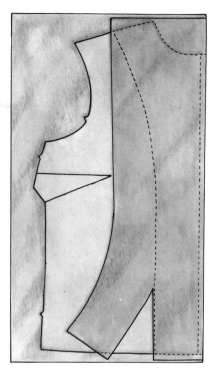

2 On the tracing of the front piece, draw a line $\frac{5}{8}$in (1.5cm) outside the center front line (marked "place on fold") and mark this as the new foldline. Fold the paper down this line and trace the front neck curve and shoulder line from the pattern. Measure in and mark points $2\frac{1}{2}$in (6.5cm) from the edge at intervals around the neck and down the fold line. Join the points, using a flexible curve around the neck edge and cut along the marked line.

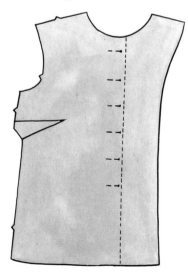

3 Mark the position of the first buttonhole with a pin, $2\frac{1}{2}$in (6.5cm) from the neck edge on the center front line. Mark the buttonhole horizontally and draw it in on the pattern, making it $\frac{1}{8}$in (3mm) wider than the button to be used and placing it so that it overlaps the center front line by $\frac{1}{8}$in (3mm). Draw in the remaining five buttonholes at $3\frac{1}{2}$in (9cm) intervals.

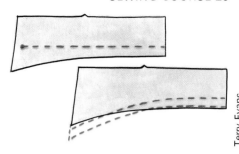

Terry Evans

4 Trace the shirt collar and mark the $\frac{5}{8}$in (1.5cm)-wide seam allowance all around. You can alter the shape of the collar by moving the collar point but keep it $\frac{5}{8}$in (1.5cm) from the front edge. For a straight collar, draw the collar point level with the seamline of the long edge as shown. Join the point to the seamline. Draw the new cutting line $\frac{5}{8}$in (1.5cm) outside the new seamline.
For a curved collar, place the point outside the existing point—but still $\frac{5}{8}$in (1.5cm) from the front edge—and join it to the seamline of the long edge, using a flexible curve. Draw in the new cutting line $\frac{5}{8}$in (1.5cm) from the seamline. The sleeve, collar band and cuff patterns are not altered for this design.

Directions for making

Suggested fabrics
Cottons, cotton blends, Viyella ® or—for more experienced dressmakers—silk.

Materials
*36in (90cm)-wide fabric with or
   without nap:
   Sizes 10, 12, 14: $3\frac{1}{8}$yd (2.8m)
   Sizes 16, 18, 20: $3\frac{1}{3}$yd (3m)
45in (115cm)-wide fabric with or
   without nap:
   Sizes 10, 12, 14: $2\frac{7}{8}$yd (2.6m)
   Sizes 16, 18, 20: 3yd (2.7m)
36in (90cm)-wide interfacing:
   Sizes 10 and 12:$\frac{7}{8}$yd (.8m)
   Sizes 14, 16, 18 and 20: $1\frac{1}{8}$yd
   (1m)
Matching sewing thread
Nine $\frac{1}{2}$in (1.3cm) buttons*

1 Alter the pattern pieces for the shirt front and collar as directed opposite and on this page.
2 Prepare the fabric and pin on the pattern pieces following the correct layout for your fabric width. Cut out the pieces following the pattern outline closely. If you are using a balanced plaid fabric, follow the directions on page 68 for preparing the fabric and cutting out.
3 Transfer all pattern markings to the fabric.
4 Remove the pattern pieces. Pin on and cut out the appropriate pattern pieces from interfacing, following the layout. The shirt front facing is cut to the foldline only, as shown by piece 1 on the layout.

Key to adjusted pattern pieces

1 Shirt front	Cut 2
2 Shirt back	Cut 1 on fold
6 Collar	Cut 2
7 Collar band	Cut 2
8 Sleeve	Cut 2
9 Cuff	Cut 2

Interfacing, use pieces 1 (see step 4 page 71), 6, 7, 9.

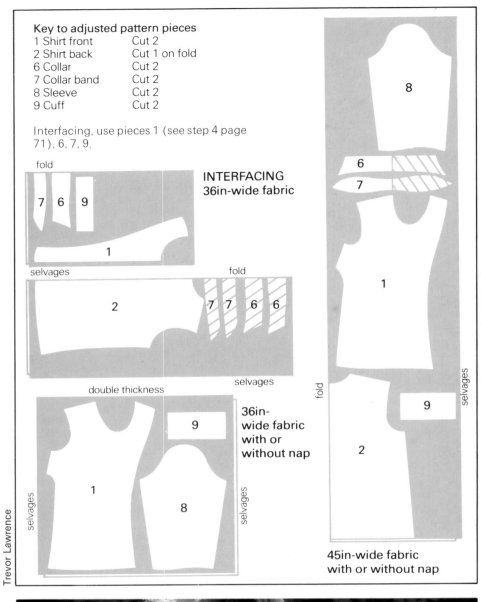

INTERFACING
36in-wide fabric

36in-wide fabric with or without nap

45in-wide fabric with or without nap

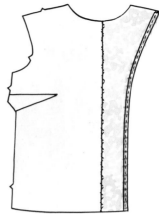

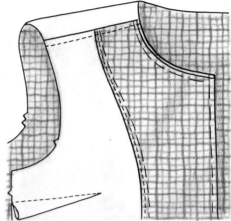

5 Iron or baste interfacing to the wrong side of the facing. Finish the facing as shown on page 69. Baste and stitch the bust darts and press them down.

6 Join the shoulder seams of the shirt, including the facing in the seam and using flat felled seams pressed to the back (see page 70).

7 Make the collar and topstitch $\frac{1}{4}$in (6mm) from the edge on the stitched sides. Attach the collar bands to the collar and stitch the collar to the shirt neck as shown in Volume 5, pages 59 and 60. Topstitch the collar band and front edges of the shirt and continuous line, working $\frac{1}{4}$in (6mm) from the edge.

Terry Evans

*Set-in shirt sleeve
*Sewing on buttons
*Making buttons
*Coordinating shirt: directions
 for making (2)

Set-in shirt sleeve

A shirt sleeve, unlike a blouse sleeve, is set into the garment with a flat felled seam. Sleeves on men's shirts are nearly always attached in this way, as flat felled seams are very· strong. The sleeve is attached to the garment after the shoulder seams have been stitched but before the side and sleeve seams have been sewn.

1 Run two rows of ease stitches around the sleeve cap between the notches, one on each side of the seamline. Pin the sleeve to the armhole edge with right sides together and the notches matching. The circle on the sleeve should be matched to the shoulder seam.

2 Pull up the ease threads so that the sleeve fits the armhole edge and the fullness is evenly distributed. Baste and stitch, with the sleeve side up on the machine.

3 Press the seam open and then press it toward the sleeve. Trim seam allowance on sleeve only, to $\frac{1}{8}$in (3mm).

4 Turn under $\frac{1}{4}$in (6mm) on the shirt seam allowance and baste it down over the trimmed seam allowance.

5 Stitch close to the fold. If you prefer, stitch on the right side, taking care to follow foldline on wrong side. Press.

Sewing on buttons

Some buttons are made with shanks— short necks which raise the button above the fabric. A shank leaves space for the part of the garment containing the buttonhole.

When sewing on this kind of button take care not to pull the stitches too tight and make sure that the button shank lines up with the buttonholes. This means that the stitches are parallel to the front edge of the garment.

To sew a button without a shank on a medium- or heavy-weight fabric, you usually make a shank with the thread, as shown opposite. This kind of button can, however, be stitched flat to the garment on very lightweight fabric, which will fit smoothly around the button even without a shank. A shank is also unnecessary if the buttons are purely decorative. The buttons can be attached by hand or machine.

Buttons without shanks

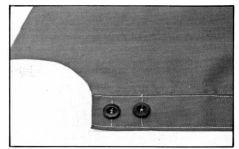

1 To sew on a button by hand, center the button over the position marked and check that it corresponds with the buttonhole. Take stitches from the wrong side of the fabric through the holes and back to the wrong side of the fabric, so that the button is securely attached. Sew in ends inconspicuously on the wrong side of the garment.

2 On buttons with four holes, the stitches can be worked either diagonally over the center of the button or in two parallel pairs of stitches.

3 To attach the button by machine, lower the feed dog and place the button below the slot in the presser foot. Lower the foot. Adjust stitch length to 0 and width to fit between the holes. Take the first stitch turning the wheel by hand to check the width, then take several stitches to secure the button.

Making a thread shank

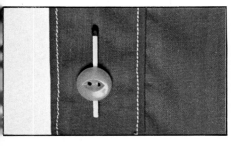

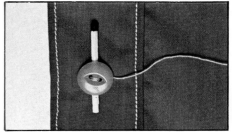

1 Position the button correctly on the garment. Slip a match between button and fabric so that the holes lie on each side of it.

2 Take the stitches attaching the button as directed above, holding the match in place while you stitch. Do not fasten the thread.

3 Remove the match and wind the thread around the vertical threads repeatedly to form a solid thread shank from fabric to button. Fasten securely.

Making buttons

Buttons which do not match the fabric can spoil the finished look of a garment.

If you have difficulty finding suitable buttons, make your own.
There are two basic ways to make buttons—either by covering flat rings or

by covering ready-made button forms. Button forms vary slightly according to the manufacturer, but the basic principles are the same for most types.

Buttons made with rings

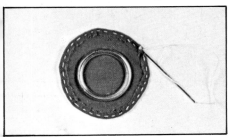

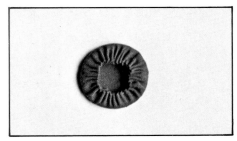

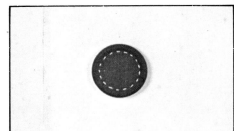

1 Use flat rings with a diameter slightly less than the buttonhole length. Cut a circle of fabric twice the diameter of ring. Turn under the raw edge of the circle and secure with a row of running stitches.

2 Pull the thread so that the fabric is gathered up at the back of the ring. Fasten the thread securely.

3 For a finishing touch, topstitch the buttons by hand close to the inner edge of the ring.

Mike Berend

Buttons made by covering button forms

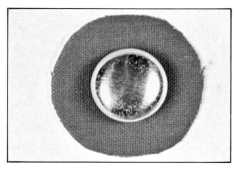

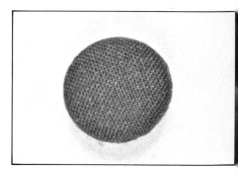

1 There are two parts to the button form: the front, slightly curved section, which may have a pronged inner edge to make the fabric easier to attach, and the back of the button, which fits exactly into the front to secure the covering. Choose a form with a diameter a little smaller than the buttonhole.

2 Cut out a circle of fabric with almost twice the diameter of the button front. Cover the front of the button with this circle of fabric (attaching it to the prongs if there are any).

3 Snap the back into the wrong side of the button so that the two pieces are firmly joined with the fabric securely held all around. The manufacturers of some button forms supply a holder and pusher to make the process easier.

Shirt: directions for making (2)

The directions that follow are for completing the shirt which was started in Sewing course 25, page 71.

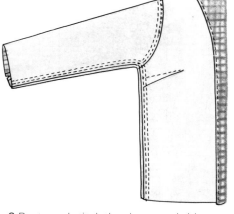

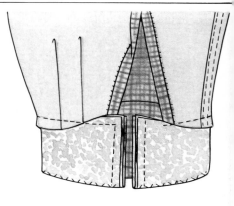

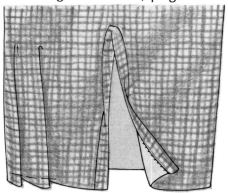

3 Baste and stitch the sleeve and side seams in one continuous line with right sides together and the notches matching. Press the seam allowances toward the back, and finish the seam to make a flat felled seam, as on the armhole.

5 Fold the cuff in half, right sides together, and stitch the short edges. Trim the seam allowances and turn the cuff right side out.

1 Make a continuous lapped opening at cuff edge of both sleeves, as shown in Sewing course 21, Volume 5, page 63. Fold and baste pleats into place as indicated.

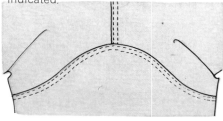

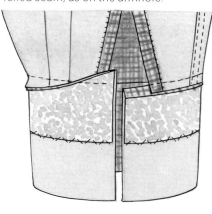

2 Set the sleeve into the armhole using a flat felled seam as directed on page 70.

4 Attach interfacing to one half of each cuff and stitch the interfaced half of the cuff to the lower sleeve edge. Grade the seam allowance and press toward the cuff.

Victor Yuan

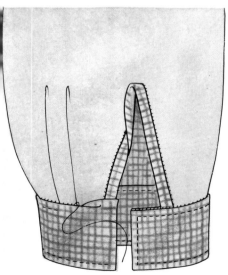

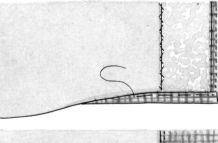

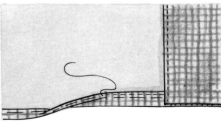

Terry Evans

6 Turn under the raw edge and slip stitch t in place on the wrong side. Topstitch he cuff ¼in (6mm) from the edge working from the right side.

7 Turn ¼in (6mm) to the wrong side at the lower edge of the shirt. Make a second hem ⅜in (1cm) wide and machine stitch it in place ¼in (6mm) from the lower hem edge. Press.

8 Make buttonholes by hand or machine on the right front and on each cuff in the positions marked. Sew the buttons to the left front and underside of each cuff to correspond with the buttonholes. Press.

Sewing / COURSE 27

Introducing smocking

Smocking is a traditional way of controlling fullness in a garment. The fabric is first gathered or pleated to the required finished width and then hand-stitched in a decorative pattern. Smocking makes an attractive detail on yokes, sleeves, pockets and necklines of dresses and shirts. It is often used on children's clothes because the smocked fabric is slightly elastic.

The most suitable fabrics for smocking are soft ones, such as gingham, cotton and wool blends, fine woolens, voile, lawn and some lightweight silks.

The amount of fabric needed in the width of a garment will depend on whether the smocking is to serve its usual, practical purpose of controlling fullness, in which case three times the width is needed, or is intended to be decorative, in which case you need only twice the finished width.

If you are adapting a pattern to include smocking, it is a good idea to make a sample first to make sure you are allowing enough fullness.

The pleating or gathering stitches are normally positioned with the help of a smocking transfer pattern. This consists of rows of evenly spaced dots and is pressed onto the wrong side of the fabric with a hot iron. If you use a fabric with even checks or stripes you may be able to use these lines as a guide; ¼in (6mm) spacing is usually sufficient.

Pearl cotton and cotton embroidery floss are the most suitable threads for smocking. Here we show you how to work three basic stitches. Others will be included in later courses.

Gathering fabric for smocking

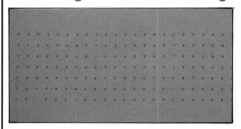 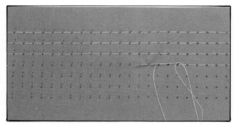 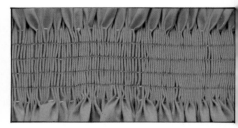

1 Cut the transfer to the exact width and depth of the area to be smocked. Position it accurately, face down on the wrong side of the fabric, leaving the seam allowances uncovered. Press over the transfer and remove it from the fabric as soon as the dots have been transferred.

2 Make each row of gathering with a separate thread, starting on the right-hand side. Knot the thread and make a back stitch at the first dot. Take the needle over the fabric and pick up the small amount of fabric covered by the second dot. Continue in this way until each row is complete, leaving the ends of the threads loose at the left-hand side.

3 Trim the ends of the threads to equal lengths and pull them up evenly but not too tightly. Knot the threads together in pairs.
Work the smocking (see samples below and opposite) over the whole area. Remove the gathering threads and press the work lightly on the wrong side with a hot iron and damp cloth.

Cable stitch

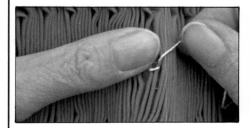 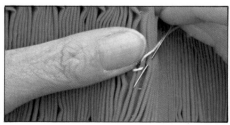 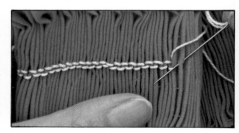

1 Working from left to right, draw the first and second pleats together, bringing the needle out between the pleats with the thread above the needle.

2 Repeat on the next pleat, but this time bring the needle out below the thread.

3 Continue to end of row, alternating "above" and "below" stitches.

Outline stitch

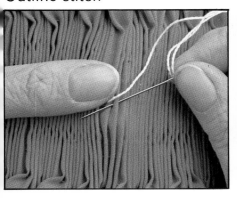

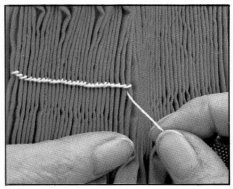

1 Work from left to right. Bring the needle up through the first pleat and into the next pleat in a slanting position, keeping the thread above the needle.

2 Pull the needle through, drawing the pleats together. Repeat to the end of the row.
This stitch controls the fullness firmly.

3 If you are doing a second row, alter the effect by keeping the thread below the needle with every stitch.

Vandyke stitch

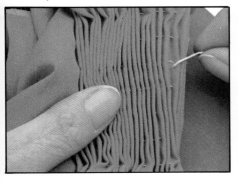

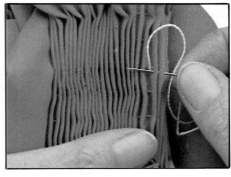

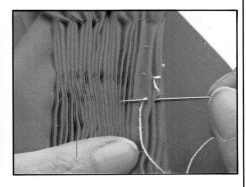

1 This stitch is sewn from right to left. Bring the needle out on the second pleat from the right, on the upper of the two rows of gathering to be used.

2 Make a back stitch through the first and second pleats, holding thread above the needle.

3 Go down to the second gathering thread and pick up the second and third pleats. Make a back stitch over them, holding the thread below the needle.

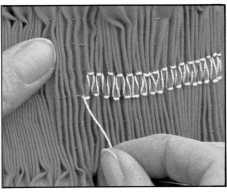

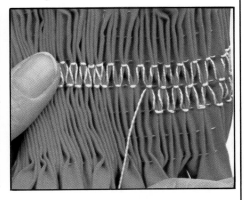

4 Return to the first gathering thread and join the third and fourth pleats in the same way, but keeping the thread above the needle.

5 Continue in this way to the end, stitching alternately on the first and second rows.

6 Start the next smocking row on the third gathering thread and move up to the second thread; but instead of making additional backstitches, simply draw the thread under the previous stitches. Start each subsequent row alternately up or down to join with the previous row.

Paul Williams

Needlework / COURSE 8

*Bargello stitch
*Bargello patterns
*Mounting a slip seat
*Bargello seat cover

Bargello

Bargello is a form of needlepoint in which a straight, vertical stitch is used to create geometric repeat designs. One of the best known of these designs is a series of zig-zag, flame-like lines across the canvas that are done in gradations of one or more colors. Because early examples were found in Florence in Italy, bargello work is sometimes also called Florentine embroidery.

In general, the same canvas, threads and needles used in other kinds of needlepoint are also used in bargello. In bargello, however, mono canvas, rather than Penelope, is always used.

Unlike other needlepoint, bargello is always worked from a graph rather tha[n] from a design marked on the canvas. Wit[h] bargello, however, it is usually possible t[o] embroider one or more foundation row[s] of stitches to establish the pattern an[d] then use these rows as a guide for addi[-]tional rows so that constant reference t[o] the graph is not necessary.

Bargello stitch

The bargello stitch is a straight, vertical stitch worked over one or more threads of the canvas. The number of threads varies according to the pattern. If a stitch is too long, however, it can catch and pull.

Work the foundation row from the center out to the sides. Then work back and forth across the canvas to the top. Reverse the canvas so that the bottom is at the top and then work from the center to the top again to finish. The top and bottom of each stitch share a hole with the ends of other stitches.

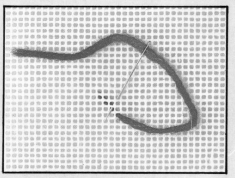

1 Bring the needle up at the bottom of first stitch. Insert it one or more holes directly above at top of stitch.

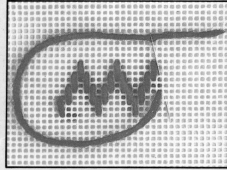

2 Bring needle up at bottom of second stitch in next vertical row of holes. Continue taking one straight vertical stitch in each vertical row of holes.

Bargello pattern 1

The traditional flamestitch pattern is easy to do. One version is shown at the right. Vary the widths and heights of the peaks to suit yourself. First, establish your foundation row by working out from the center in one direction, then the other. This ensures that your pattern is centered. Now, working from one edge to the other, stitch another row just above the first in a slightly lighter or darker version of the same color. After you have done rows in several color gradations, switch to another color and repeat the process before returning to the original color. Continue to the top of the canvas, turn, and finish.

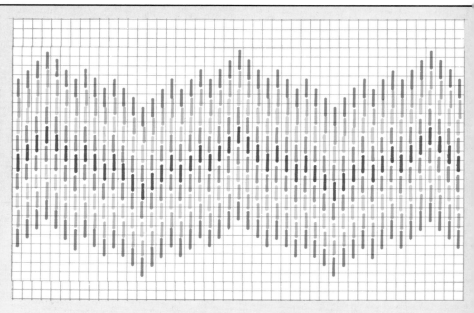

Simon Butcher

The bargello stitch can be used for a wide variety of items.

Bargello pattern 2

In this repeat pattern, the bargello stitch is used to create geometric shapes as well as lines. The design is more complex and requires closer attention to the graph until the pattern is well established. Begin in the middle and embroider a green diagonal line out toward each corner. Add the other green diagonal lines. Then fill in the diamond shapes created by the lines.

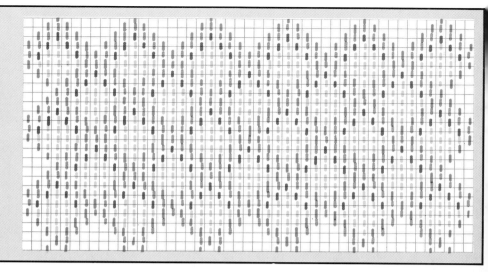

Mounting a slip seat

1 Remove seat from chair (there may be screws underneath holding it). You may also remove old cover from seat. Measure seat horizontally and vertically at its widest. Cut out a rectangle of muslin about 3in (7.5cm) larger all around than the seat at its largest.

2 Mark horizontal and vertical lines across the center of the seat with a pencil or basting stitches. Mark horizontal and vertical lines through the center of the muslin rectangle. Matching lines, pin muslin to seat from center out along the center lines and then along the edges, making folds at the corners. Mark muslin with a pencil along each side of each fold and along the edges. Remove muslin and cut out pattern along lines indicating edges and corners.

3 Prepare a piece of canvas 3-4in (8-10 cm) larger all around than the largest dimensions of the muslin pattern (see Volume 1, page 71). Center pattern on canvas by matching horizontal and vertical lines and pin in place. Trace around the muslin pattern on canvas with a pencil. Remove muslin.
The needlepoint stitches should fill the area within these lines and extend 1in (2.5cm) beyond them along the 4 side edges. Added areas of stitching will extend under seat when cover is mounted.

4 After embroidered canvas is blocked, stitch around edges of embroidery and cut off taped edges. Lay canvas face down and place seat wrong side up on top matching horizontal and vertical lines. Pull side edges of canvas over edges of seat and hammer upholstery tacks through centers to wood frame.

5 Fold excess canvas at corners in neat pleats, bringing needlepointed edges together. Tack to hold in place. Continue tacking in the middle of each empty space around the edge of the needlepoint until the tacks are about 1in (2.5cm) apart. Sew corners by hand.

6 Place seat right side up on backing material and trace around it. Cut out backing. Turn under 1in (2.5cm) around edges, baste and press. Place over back of seat with edges meeting needlepoint edges. Tack in place.

Splendid seating

Cover a slip seat in easy bargello stitch and a traditional flame
stitch pattern. Or use the same stitch in a geometric design.

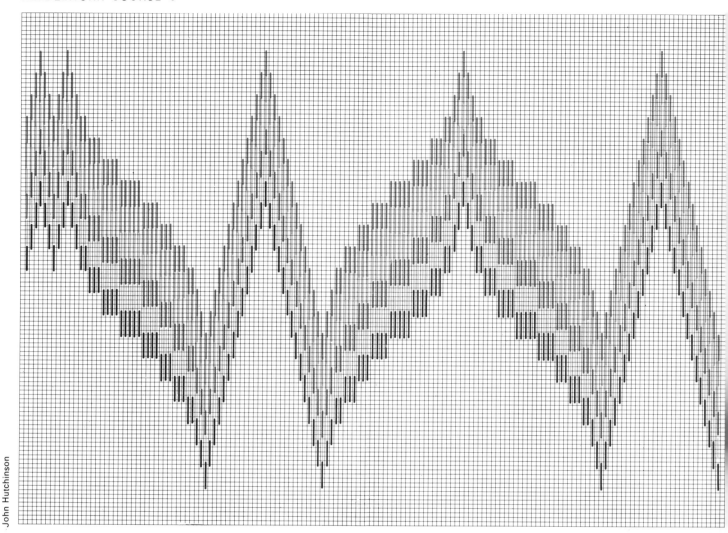

John Hutchinson

Note: The seat we covered measured 17 x 19in (43 x 48cm) at its widest and deepest. The materials we used are listed below. To determine what you will need, measure your seat and decide what pattern, gauge of canvas, and thread you wish to use. Then ask an experienced salesperson in a needlework shop or department to estimate the amounts for you.

Materials
> *Tapemeasure*
> *Unbleached muslin (a piece about 6in [15cm] longer and wider than the seat cover*
> *Yardstick*
> *Pencil*
> *Basting thread and needle (optional)*
> *Scissors*
> *Needlepoint canvas (we used No. 18)*
> *Masking tape*
> *Straight pins*
> *Wool embroidery thread—we used 3 strands of crewel wool — a total of about 9oz (250g) divided equally among 6 colors*

> *Tapestry needle (we used No. 20)*
> *Board for blocking*
> *Brown paper*
> *Plastic spray bottle or sponge*
> *Thumbtacks or push pins*
> *Hammer*
> *Sewing thread to stitch canvas*
> *Upholstery tacks*
> *Backing material (a piece large enough to cover the bottom of seat)*

To make
1 Remove seat from chair (or bench) and measure. Remove a corner of the old cover to see if there is an undercover. If there is, you may wish to remove the old cover. If not, leave the old cover on.
2 Make a muslin pattern (see page 82).
3 Prepare a piece of canvas at least 6in (15cm) wider and longer than the muslin pattern (see Volume 1, page 71).
4 Center the muslin pattern on the canvas, pin and trace around it (see page 82). Remove the muslin pattern and extend the side edges of the seat shape out 1in (2.5cm). The needlepoint should fill these side extensions as well as the seat shape.

The pattern above is for the right half of the chair seat. The left half is the mirror image of it.

5 Begin bargello stitches in the center of the canvas. Work a foundation row out to the right side of the area to be stitched and then to the left side. Only half of the pattern we used is shown above. The vertical row at the left on the pattern is the center row on the seat. If you use the pattern for your seat, start in the center of your canvas and work out to the right, using as much of the pattern as you need or extending it by adding part or all of another broad peak. Then work from the center out to the left side of your canvas, following the same pattern from the vertical row next to the center out to the side. The left side of your canvas should be a mirror image of the right side.
6 Work from the foundation row to the top of the area to be stitched on the canvas. Then turn the canvas so the bottom is at the top and work to the top again to finish the needlepoint.
7 Block canvas (see Volume 1, page 72).
8 Mount seat cover (see page 82).

CROCHET

Like father . . . like son

Textured Aran-style stitches have been used to form panels on the front and sleeves of these sweaters. They are worked in a traditional Aran yarn for warmth.

Sizes

To fit 28[30:32:34:36:38:40]in (71[76:83:87:92:97:102]cm) chest. Length, 18[19¾:21:22½:23¾:25:26]in (46[50:54:57:60:63:66]cm). Sleeve seam, 14[16:17:17¾:18:18½:19]in (36[40:43:45:46:47:48]cm).

Note Directions for larger sizes are in brackets []; where there is only one set of figures it applies to all sizes.

Materials

20[22:23:27:29:30:34]oz (550[600: 650:750:800:850:950]g) of a knitting worsted
Sizes F and H (4.00 and 5.00mm) crochet hooks

Gauge

14hdc to 4in (10cm) on size H (5.00mm) hook.

Back

Using size F (4.00mm) hook make 55[59: 63:67:71:75:79]ch.
Base row (RS) 1dc into 4th ch from hook, 1dc into each ch to end. Turn. 53[57:61: 65:69:73:77]sts.
1st ribbing row 3ch to count as first dc, *insert hook from back of work around stem of next dc, yo and draw a loop through, complete as for a dc—called raised dc at back (RDB)—, insert hook from front of work around stem of next dc, yo and draw a loop through, complete as for a dc—called raised dc at front (RDF)—, rep from * to last 2 sts, RDB around next dc, 1dc into turning ch. Turn.
2nd ribbing row 3ch, *RDF around next dc, RDB around next dc, rep from * to last 2 sts, RDF around next dc, 1dc into

turning ch. Turn. Rep these 2 rows until work measures 1½[1½:2:2:2:2¼:2¼]in (4[4:5:5:5:6:6]cm) from beg; end with first row **. Change to size H (5.00mm) hook. Beg patt.

1st row 2ch to count as first hdc, 1hdc into each st to end. Turn. Cont in hdc until work measures 11[12¼:13:13¾:14¼: 15:15¼]in (28[31:33:35:36:38:39]cm) from beg; end with WS row.
Shape armholes
Next row Sl st over first 3 sts, patt to last 2 sts, turn. Rep last row once more. Dec one st at each end of next and foll 1[1:2:2:3:3:4] rows. 41[45:47:51:53:57: 59] sts. Cont straight until armholes measure 7[7½:8:8¾:9½:10:10¾]in (18[19:21:22:24:25:27]cm), end with WS row.
Shape shoulders
Next row Sl st over next 4[5:5:5:6:6:6] sts, patt to last 3[4:4:4:5:5:5] sts, turn. Rep last row once more.
Next row Sl st over first 5[4:5:6:5:6:7] sts, patt to last 4[3:4:5:4:5:6] sts, turn. 21[23:23:25:25:27:27] sts rem for neck. Fasten off.

Front

Work as for back to ** Change to size H (5.00mm) hook. Beg patt.
1st row 2ch, 1hdc into each of next 16[18:19:21:23:24:26] sts, RDF around each of next 4 sts, 1hdc into each of next 11[11:13:13:13:15:15] sts, RDF around each of next 4 sts, 1hdc into each of next 17[19:20:22:24:25:27] sts. Turn.
2nd row 2ch, 1hdc into each of next 15[17:18:20:22:23:25] sts, RDB around each of next 4 sts, 1hdc into each of next

13[13:15:15:15:17:17] sts RDB around next 4 sts, 1hdc into each st to end. Turn.
3rd row 2ch, 1hdc into each of next 14[16:17:19:21:22:24] sts, RDF around each of next 4 sts, 1hdc into each of next 7[7:8:8:8:9:9] sts, (yo, insert hook into next st, yo and draw a loop through) 4 times into same st, yo and draw through all 9 loops on hook—called make bobble or MB, 1hdc into each of next 7[7:8:8:8:9:9] sts, RDF around each of next 4 sts, 1hdc into each st to end. Turn.
4th row 2ch, 1hdc into each of next 13[15:16:18:20:21:23] sts, RDB around each of next 4 sts, 1hdc into each of next 17[17:19:19:19:21:21] sts, RDB around next 4 sts, 1hdc into each st to end. Turn.
5th row 2ch, 1hdc into each of next 12[14:15:17:19:20:22] sts, RDF around each of next 4 sts, 1hdc into each of next 6[6:7:7:7:8:8] sts, MB, 1hdc into each of next 5 sts, MB, 1hdc into each of next 6[6:7:7:7:8:8] sts, RDF around each of next 4 sts, 1hdc into each st to end. Turn.

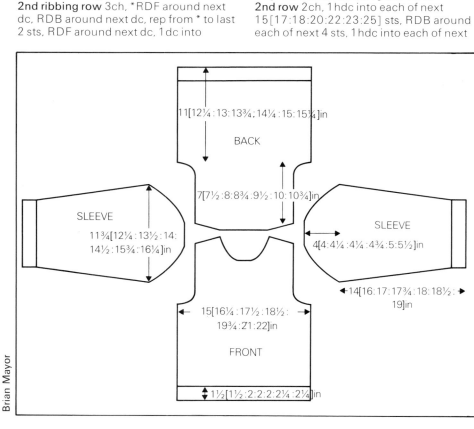

BACK

11[12¼:13:13¾:14¼:15:15¼]in

7[7½:8:8¾:9½:10:10¾]in

SLEEVE
11¾[12¼:13½:14: 14½:15¾:16¼]in

SLEEVE
4[4:4¼:4¼:4¾:5:5½]in

14[16:17:17¾:18:18½: 19]in

15[16¼:17½:18½: 19¾:21:22]in

FRONT

1½[1½:2:2:2:2¼:2¼]in

6th row As 4th.
7th row As 3rd.
8th row As 2nd.
Rep these 8 rows until work is as long as back to underarm; end with WS row.
Shape armholes
Work as for back armhole shaping until 41[45:47:51:53:57:59] sts rem. Cont straight until armholes measure 4¾[5:5½: 6:6¼:6¾:7]in (12[13:14:15:16:17:18]cm) from beg; end with WS row.
Shape neck
Next row Patt over first 15[17:18:19:20: 22:23]sts, turn.
Next row Sl st over first 3 sts, patt to end. Turn.
***Dec one st at neck edge on next 3[4:4:4:5:5] rows. 10[11:12:13:14: 15:16] sts. Cont straight until armhole measures same as back to shoulder; end at armhole edge.
Shape shoulder
Next row Sl st over first 4[5:5:5:6:6:6] sts, patt to end. Turn.

Ray Duns

Next row Patt to last 3[4:4:4:5:5:5] sts, turn. 4[3:4:5:4:5:6] sts rem. Fasten off. Skip center 11[11:11:13:13:13:13] sts, rejoin yarn and patt to end.
Next row Patt to last 2 sts, turn. Finish as for first side from *** to end.

Sleeves
Using size F (4.00mm) hook make 23[25:25:27:29:31:31] ch. Work as for back to **. 21[23:23:25:27:29:29] sts. Change to size H (5.00mm) hook. Work 2 rows hdc.
3rd row 2ch, 1hdc into edge st at base of ch, 1hdc into each of next 9[10:10:11: 12:13:13] sts, MB, 1hdc into each st to last st, 2hdc into last st. Turn.
4th row 1hdc into each st to end. Turn.
5th row 2ch, 1hdc into each of next 7[8:8:9:10:11:11] sts, MB, 1hdc into each of next 5 sts, MB, 1hdc into each st to end. Turn.
6th row 2ch, 1hdc into st at base of ch, 1hdc into each st to last st, 2hdc into last st. Turn.
7th row 2ch, 1hdc into each of next 11[12:12:13:14:15:15] sts, MB, 1hdc into each st to end. Turn.
8th row 2ch, 1hdc into each st to end. Turn.
Cont in patt as set, working bobbles in center, inc one st at each end of next and every foll 3rd row until there are 41[43:47:49:51:55:57] sts. Cont straight until sleeve measures 14[16:17: 17¾:18:18½:19]in (36[40:43:45:46: 47:48]cm) from beg; end with WS row.
Shape top
Dec one st at each end of next 7[7:8:8:8: 9:10] rows, then 2 sts at each end of foll 4[4:4:4:5:5:5] rows. 11[13:15:17: 15:17:19] sts rem. Fasten off.

Neckband
Join right shoulders. With size F (4.00mm) hook and RS facing, work 12[13:13: 14:14:15:15] sc down left front neck, 11[11:11:13:13:13:13] sc across front neck, 13[14:14:15:15:16:16] sc up right front neck and 21[23:23:25:25:27:27] sc across back. 1 row in dc. Rep 2 ribbing rows as for waistband until neckband measures ¾[¾:1:1:1:1½:1½]in (2[2:3:3:3: 4:4]cm). Fasten off.

To finish
Surface crochet Outline bobble panels using doubled yarn. Beg at first patt row on front and sleeves, join yarn to st under first bobble and work zig-zag lines, moving two sts to left and right to enclose 4 bobbles in diamond shape. Lines cross on a first patt row immediately above and below 2 single bobbles. For man's sweater, outline each side of diamond shapes—with 2 background sts between—with separate zig-zag line. Join left shoulder and neckband seam. Set in sleeves. Join side and sleeve seams. Press seams.

Technique tip
Working surface crochet
Surface crochet is, as the name suggests, worked on the surface of the finished fabric. It is often used on Aran designs to produce a clear, three-dimensional effect. It has been used to outline the groups of bobbles on these sweaters with diamonds. To work surface crochet, begin by joining the yarn to the lower edge of the fabric. With the right side of the work facing, insert the hook from the front to the back through the fabric. Holding the yarn at the back of the work, wrap the yarn over the hook and draw a loop through the fabric. With the loop still on the hook, insert the hook through the fabric a short distance from where the hook was first inserted. Wrap the yarn over the hook and draw a loop through the fabric and through the loop on the hook. This completes the first surface crochet chain. Continue to make chain stitches through the fabric in the same way.
Below, surface crochet is being worked over half double crochet. The yarn is being used double as instructed in the finishing directions for the Aran sweaters. The surface crochet sloping to the right is moved two stitches to the right on every row and the surface crochet sloping to the left is moved two stitches to the left on every row.

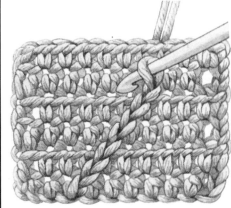

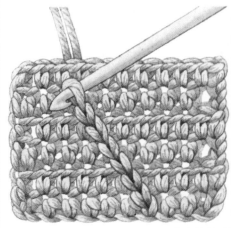

CROCHET

Rich shades of black and gold combine in these jet-set bikinis. Make them both and be a pool-side sensation.

Gold dust and ebony

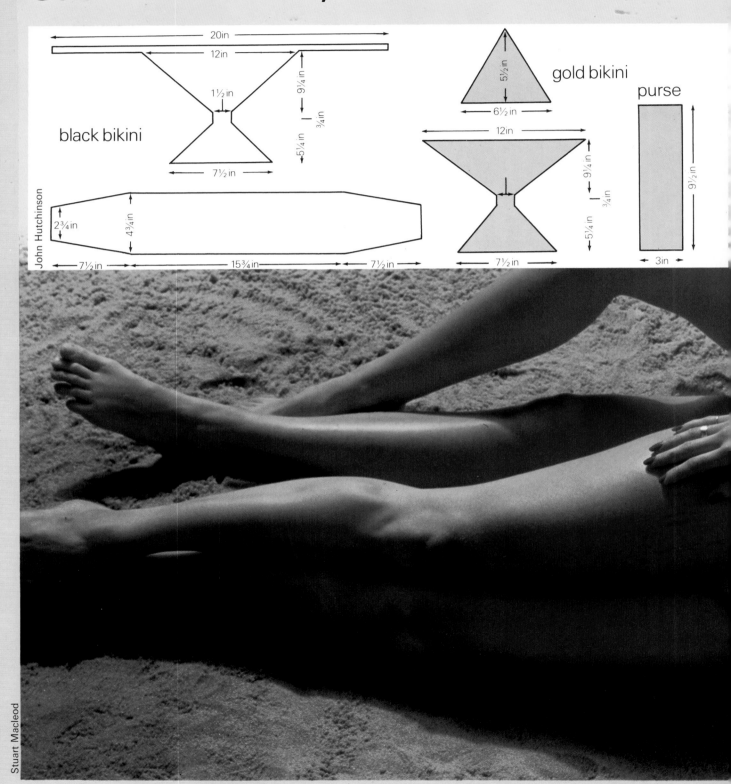

20in

12in

1½ in

9¼ in

¾ in

5¼ in

7½ in

black bikini

5½ in

6½ in

gold bikini

12in

9¼ in

¾ in

5¼ in

7½ in

purse

9½ in

3in

2¾ in

4¾ in

7½ in

15¾ in

7½ in

John Hutchinson

Stuart Macleod

old bikini

ze

o fit 32/34in (83/87cm) bust, 34/36in
37/92cm) hips.

aterials

5oz (120g) of a medium-weight
    mercerized crochet cotton in main
    color (A)
1oz (20g) in contrasting color (B)
No. 0 (2.00mm) crochet hook

auge

4sc and 16 rows to 1½in (4cm).

kini bottom

sing No. 0 (2.00mm) hook and A, make
1ch for top edge of back.
ase row 1sc into 3rd ch from hook, 1sc
to each ch to end. Turn. 110 sts.
nt in sc dec 1 sc at beg of every
w, by skipping 1sc, until 12 sts rem.
ork 8 rows without shaping, then inc
sc at beg of every row, by working 1sc
to first sc, until there are 68 sts.

Edging

Work a row of sc around outer edge of
panties working 3sc at each corner and
joining last sc to first with sl st. Join on B.
Work 1sc into each sc around outer edge
and at each corner work 90ch, sl st into
each ch to form ties, join last sc to first
with a sl st. Fasten off. Knot ends of ties.

Top

Using No. 0 (2.00mm) hook and A, make
60ch.
Base row 1sc into 3rd ch from hook, 1sc
into each ch to end. Turn. 59 sts.
Cont in sc dec 1 sc at beg of every row
until one st remains. Work a row of sc
evenly around outer edge, join last sc to

first with sl st. Fasten off. Make another
piece the same way.

Edging

Using No. 0 (2.00mm) hook and B, make
150ch, sl st into each ch to end for first
tie, now work 1sc into each sc along
lower edge of one triangle, 5ch, 1sc
into each sc along lower edge of other
triangle, make 150ch, sl st into each ch
for 2nd tie, now work *1sc into each sc
along side of triangle, make 150ch, sl st
into each ch for neck tie, 1 sc into each
sc along other side of triangle, * sl st into
each of the 15ch at center, rep from * to *
sl st into first sc at lower edge. Fasten off

Purse (made in one piece)
Using No. 0 (2.00mm) hook and A, make 27ch.
Base row 1sc into 3rd ch from hook, 1sc into each ch to end. Turn.
Patt row 2ch to count as first sc, 1sc into each to end. Turn.
Rep patt row 98 times, chain 140, sl st into each ch to end for tie. Fold purse in half crosswise and working through double thickness work 1sc into each row end along side edge, 3sc into corner, 1sc into each sc along fold, 3sc into corner, then 1sc into each row end along other side edge, work 140ch, sl st into each ch for tie. Fasten off.

Black bikini

Size
As gold bikini.

Materials
6oz (160g) of a medium-weight mercerized cotton in main color (A)
1oz (20g) in contrasting color (B)
No. 0 (2.00mm) crochet hook
Elastic thread
3 hooks and eyes

Gauge
14sc and 16 rows to 1½in (4cm).

Bikini bottom
Using No. 0 (2.00mm) hook and A, chain 187 for top edge of back and straps.
Base row 1sc into 3rd ch from hook, 1sc into each ch to end. Turn. 186 sts.
Next row 2 ch to count as first sc, 1 sc into each st to end. Turn. Rep last row once more. Cut off yarn.
Skip first 38sc, for side strap, rejoin yarn to next sc, 2ch, 1sc into each sc to within last 38sc, turn.
Cont in sc decreasing 1sc at beg of every row, by skipping 1sc, until 12 sts remain. Work 8 rows without shaping, then inc 1sc at beg of every row, by working 1sc into first sc, until there are 68 sts.
Work 3 rows without shaping. Fasten off.
Sew side bands to front.
Join on A and work a row of sc evenly around outer edge. Cut off A; join B and work 1sc into each sc around outer edge. Fasten off.
Run 2 rows of elastic thread around top.

Top
Using No. 0 (2.00mm) hook and A, chain 27.
Base row 1sc into 3rd ch from hook, 1sc into each ch to end. Turn. 26 sts.
Next row 2ch to count as first sc, 1sc into each sc to end. Turn. Rep last row 5 times more.
Inc 1 sc at each end of next and every foll 8th row until there are 44 sts.
Work 168 rows without shaping. Dec 1sc at each end of next and every foll 8th row until 26sc remain. Work 7 rows without shaping. Do not turn on last row but work a row of sc around outer edge working 3 sc at each corner. Cut off A; join on B and work 1 sc into each sc around outer edge. Fasten off.

Tie
Using No. 0 (2.00mm) hook and B, chain 350, sl st into each ch to end. Fasten off. Sew 3 hooks and eyes to ends to fasten. Knot tie around center of band.

Stuart Macleod

KNITTING

Lacy and lovely

Dress your baby in this pretty party dress embroidered at
random with dainty flowers.

Belinda

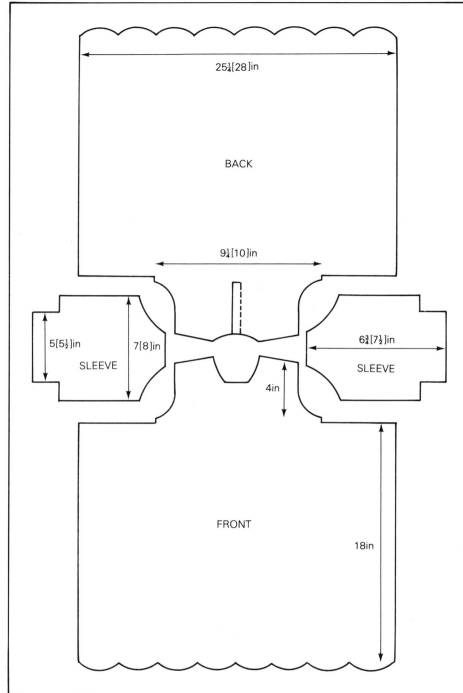

BACK

25¼[28]in

9¼[10]in

SLEEVE

5[5½]in

7[8]in

6¾[7½]in

SLEEVE

4in

FRONT

18in

John Hutchinson

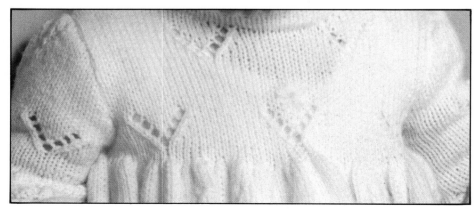

Sizes
To fit 18[20]in (46[51]cm) chest.
Length, 22½in (57cm).
Sleeve seam, 6[6¾]in (15[17]cm)

Note Directions for the larger size are in brackets []; where there is only one set of figures, it applies to both sizes.

Gauge
26 sts and 34 rows to 4in (10cm) in st st on No. 3 (3¼mm) needles.

Materials
12[14]oz (320[380]g) of a sport yarn in main color (A)
1½oz [40g] in contrasting colors (B, C and D)
One pair No. 3 (3¼mm) knitting needles
4 small buttons

Front
Using No. 3 (3¼mm) needles and B, cast on 164[182] sts. K one row and beg zigzag patt as foll:
1st row (RS) K1, (K2 tog) 3 times, * (yo, K1) 6 times, (K2 tog) 6 times, rep from * to last 13 sts, (yo, K1) 6 times, (K2 tog) 3 times, K1.
2nd row P to end.
3rd row P to end.
4th row Join in A and P to end.
5th row As first row.
6th row As 2nd row.
7th row As 3rd row.
8th row Join in C and P to end.
These 8 rows form zigzag patt, cont in patt changing color every 4 rows in the sequence of 4 rows C, 4 rows A, 4 rows D, 4 rows A, 4 rows B, 4 rows A, 4 rows C, 4 rows A, 4 rows D, then change to A and work 3 rows of patt only, work 8 rows in st st, then beg eyelet patt as foll:
1st row K18, * yo, sl 1, K1, psso, K16, rep from * to last 2 sts, K2.
2nd and every other row P to end.
3rd row K16, * K2 tog, yo, K1, yo, sl 1, K1, psso, K13, rep from * to last 4 sts, K4.
5th row K15, * K2 tog, yo, K3, yo, sl 1, K1, psso, K11, rep from * to last 5 sts, K5.
7th row K14, * K2 tog, yo, K5, yo, sl 1, K1, psso, K9, rep from * to last 6 sts, K6.
8th row P to end.
Work 10 rows in st st.
19th row K9, * yo, sl 1, K1, psso, K16, rep from *, ending last rep K9.
20th and every other row P to end.
21st row K7, * K2 tog, yo, K1, yo, sl 1, K1, psso, K13, rep from *, ending last rep K8.
23rd row K6, * K2 tog, yo, K3, yo, sl 1, K1, psso, K11, rep from *, ending last rep K7.
25th row K5, * K2 tog, yo, K5, yo, sl 1, K1, psso, K9, rep from *, ending last rep K6.
26th row P to end.
Work 10 rows st st, beg with a K row.
These 36 rows form eyelet patt, rep until skirt measures 18in (46cm) from beg, ending with a WS row.
Next row (K2 tog) 8[5] times, (K3 tog)

Technique Tip

To work lazy daisy stitch, thread a tapestry needle with a contrasting color. Secure one end firmly at the back of the work. Bring the point to the right side. This point is the center of the flower. Insert the needle a few rows from the center without pulling the needle through, wrap the yarn around the needle loosely. Secure this loop with a neat stitch. One petal is now complete. Continue around working as many petals as desired.

44[54] times, (K2 tog) 8[5] times. 60[64] sts.

Work 3 rows in st st. Cont in patt as foll:

Next row K11[13], * yo, sl 1, K1, psso, K16, rep from *, ending last rep K11[13].

Next row P to end.

Shape armholes

Cont in patt as for skirt and keeping patt correct, shape armholes as foll:

Bind off 2 sts at beg of next 2 rows, then dec 1 st at each end of every other row until 52[56] sts rem.

Cont in patt until front measures 21¼in (54cm) from beg, ending with a WS row.

Shape neck

Next row Work across 21[23] sts in patt, turn leaving rem sts on a spare needle.

Keeping armhole edge even, dec 1 st at neck edge on every row until 16[18] sts rem.

Cont working even until front measures 22½in (57cm) from beg, ending at armhole edge.

Shape shoulders

Bind off 4 sts at beg of next row and every other row twice more.

Work 1 row. Bind off rem 4 [6] sts.

Rejoin yarn to sts on spare needle and work 1 row in patt.

Next row P across 21[23] sts, P2 tog, turn leaving rem 10 sts on spare needle.

Work to match first side of neck, reversing all shapings.

Back

Work as for the front to armhole shaping.

Next row Bind off 2 sts, work across 28[30] sts (including 1 st on needle), turn leaving rem sts on spare needle.

Cast on 4 sts at beg of next row for the button band.

Work these 4 sts in g st throughout for the button band.

Dec 1 st at armhole edge on every other row twice.

Work even until back measures same as front to beg of shoulder shaping.

Shape neck and shoulders

Bind off 4 sts at beg of next row, 9 sts at beg of next row (neck edge), 4 sts at beg of next row, 5 sts at beg of next row, 4 sts at beg of next row.

Work 1 row. Bind off rem 4[6] sts. Rejoin yarn to sts on spare needle.

Cast on 4 sts at beg of first row for buttonhole band.

Work to match first side of back, working a buttonhole on the 5th (RS row) and every foll 8th row as foll:

Buttonhole row K2, yo, K2 tog, work to end.

Sleeves

Using No. 3 (3¼mm) needles and A, cast on 32[36] sts and work in st st for 6 rows.

Next row K1, * yo, K2 tog. rep from *, ending with K1. Work 7 more rows in st st.

Inc row K2, (inc in next st, K1) 14[16] times, K2. 46[52] sts.

Work 9 rows in st st.

Then work in patt as for front beg first patt row with K13[16] and working all foll rows to correspond.

Work even until sleeve measures 6¾[7½]in (17[19]cm) from beg.

Shape sleeve cap

Bind off 2 sts at beg of next 4 rows.

Dec 1 st at each end of next row and then every other row 5 times. 26[32] sts.

Bind off 3 sts at beg of next 4 rows.

Bind off rem 14[20] sts.

Neckband

Sew shoulder seams. Using A, pick up and K 59 sts around neck. Work 5 rows in st st, ending with WS row.

Picot row K1, * yo, K2 tog, rep from * to end.

Work 5 more rows in st st.

Bind off loosely.

To finish

Fold neckband to WS and sew in place. Sew side and sleeve seams. Fold sleeve hems to WS and sew in place. Set in sleeves, gathering any fullness at top. Sew on buttons to correspond with buttonholes. Embroider flowers in lazy daisy stitch at random as shown in Technique Tip.

Serge Krouglikoff

EXTRA SPECIAL KNITTING

Big softie

Snuggle up in this pretty pastel turtleneck. The yarn is used double to give a rich textured look.

Sizes
To fit 32[34:36:38]in (83[87:92:97]cm) bust.
Length, 22½[22½:24:24]in (57[57:61: 61]cm).
Sleeve seam, 17[17:18:18]in (43[43: 45.5:45.5]cm).
Note Directions for larger sizes are in brackets []; if there is only one set of figures it applies to all sizes.

Materials
16[18:20:22]oz (450[500:550: 600]g) of a knitting worsted
1 pair each Nos. 8 and 10 (5¼ and 6½mm) knitting needles
1 set of four No. 7 (5mm) double-pointed needles

Gauge
14 sts and 18 rows to 4in (10cm) in patt on No. 10 (6½mm) needles, using yarn double.
Note Yarn is used double throughout.

Back
Using No. 8 (5½mm) needles and yarn double, cast on 58[62:62:70]sts.
1st ribbing row (K2, P2) to last 2 sts, K2.
2nd ribbing row (P2, K2) to last 2 sts, P2.
Rep these 2 rows for 2½in (6.5cm), ending with 2nd row, for 1st and 4th sizes dec one st at end of last row and for 2nd and 3rd sizes inc one st at end of last row.
All sizes 57[63:63:69] sts. Change to No. 10 (6½mm) needles. Beg patt.
1st row (RS) K1, *K1, yo, K2 tog tbl, K1, K2 tog, yo, rep from * to last 2 sts, K2.
2nd row K1, P2, *yo, P3 tog, yo, P3, rep from * to end, finishing last rep P2, K1.
3rd row K to end.
4th row K1, *P1, P2 tog tbl, yo, P1, yo,

P2 tog, rep from * to last 2 sts, P1, K1.
5th row K1, K2 tog, *yo, K3, yo, K3 tog, rep from * to last 6 sts, yo, K3, yo, K2 tog tbl, K1.
6th row P to end.
These 6 rows form patt. Cont in patt until work measures 15[15:15½:15½]in (38[38:39.5:39.5]) from beg; end with WS row. Place marker at each end of last row for beg of armholes. Cont in patt until work measures 7½[7½:8½:8½]in (19[19:21.5:21.5]cm) from markers; end with WS row.
Next row Work 20 sts for shoulder, bind off next 17[23:23:29] sts for neck, work to end for shoulder.
Next row Bind off first 20 sts, cut off yarn. Rejoin yarn to neck edge of rem sts, bind off these sts.

Front
Using No. 8 (5½mm) needles and yarn double, cast on 62[62:70:70] sts. Work 2 ribbing rows for 2½in (6.5cm); end with 2nd row, for 1st and 2nd sizes inc one st at end of last row and for 3rd and 4th sizes dec one st at end of last row.
All sizes 63[63:69:69] sts. Change to No. 10 (6½mm) needles. Cont in patt as for back until work measures 15[15:15½: 15½]in (38[38:39.5:39.5]cm) from beg; end with WS row. Place marker at each end of last row for beg of armholes. Cont in patt until work measures 5[5:5½:5½]in (13[13:14:14]cm) from markers; end with WS row.

Divide for neck
Next row Patt 25, turn and leave rem sts on spare needle. Dec one st at neck edge on next 5 rows. Cont in patt until work measures 7½[7½:8½:8½]in (19[19:21.5: 21.5]cm) from marker, end at side edge. Bind off. With RS facing join yarn to inner end of sts on spare needle, bind off 13[13: 19:19] sts, patt to end of row. Complete to match first side.

Sleeves
Using No. 8 (5½mm) needles and yarn double, cast on 30[30:34:34] sts. Work 2 ribbing rows for 3in (7.5cm), end with 1st row.
Inc row P1 [1:2:2], P twice into each of next 27[27:29:29] sts, P2[2:3:3]. 57[57:63:63] sts. Change to No. 10 (6½mm) needles. Work in patt as for back until work measures 17[17:18:18]in (43[43:45.5:45.5]cm). Bind off.

Turtleneck collar
Join shoulders. With RS facing, using 3 needles of set and yarn double, pick up and K 68[72:80:84] sts around neck. Work in rounds of K2, P2 ribbing for 7[7:8:8]in (18[18:20.5:20.5]cm). Bind off in ribbing.

To finish
Sew sleeves to armholes. Join side and sleeve seams. Press seams lightly.

sleeve

sleeve

5[5:5½:5½]in

7½[7½:8½:8½]in

3in

14[14:15:15]in

15[15:15½:15½]in

Brian Mayor

Thoroughbred

Wear this smart suit with a silk shirt for special occasions, or with a turtleneck sweater and scarf for a more casual look. It has a patterned yoke and a skirt flared from the hips.

Sizes
Jacket To fit 32[34:36:38]in (83[87:92:97]cm) bust. Length, 27½in (70cm). Sleeve seam, 17½in (44cm).
Skirt To fit 34[36:38:40]in (87[92:97:102]cm) hips. Length, 29½in (75cm).

Note Directions for larger sizes are in brackets []; where there is only one set of figures it applies to all sizes.

Materials
27[27:29:29]oz (750[750:800:800]g) of a sport yarn
1 pair each Nos. 2, 3, 4 and 5 (3, 3¼ 3¾ and 4mm) knitting needles
Cable needle
Waist length of 1in (2.5cm)-wide elastic for skirt

Gauge
30 sts to 4in (10cm) in main patt on No. 5 (4mm) needles.
35 sts to 4in (10cm) in yoke patt on No. 2 (3mm) needles.

Jacket

Back
Using No. 5 (4mm) needles cast on 126[134:138:146] sts. Beg main patt.
1st row P1, *K2, P2, rep from * to last st, K1.
2nd row K2, *P2, K2, rep from * to end.
Rep these 2 rows until work measures 21¼in (54cm) from beg, ending with a 2nd row and inc one st at each end of last row on 1st and 3rd sizes only. 128[134:140:146] sts. Cut off yarn and leave sts on a spare needle.
Yoke edging
Using No. 2 (3mm) needles cast on 126[132:138:144] sts. K 11 rows.
Join yoke edging to back by placing WS of yoke edging to RS of back and using No. 2 (3mm) needles K one st from back, *K one st from back tog with one st from yoke edging, rep from * to last st on back, K1. 128[134:140:146] sts.
Next row K to end.

Next row P3, *K2, P4, rep from * to last 5 sts, K2, P3.
Beg yoke patt.
1st row K3, *sl next st onto cable needle and leave at back of work, P1, then P the st from cable needle, K4, rep from * to end, but finish last rep K3 instead of K4.
2nd row P2, *sl next st onto cable needle and leave at back of work, K1, then P the st from cable needle, sl next st onto cable needle and leave at front of work, P1 then K the st from cable needle, P2, rep from * to end.
3rd row K1, *sl next st onto cable needle and leave at front of work, P1, then K the st from cable needle, K2, sl next st onto cable needle and leave at back of work, K1, then P the st from cable needle, rep from * to last st, P1.
4th row P1, K1, P4, *sl next st onto cable needle and leave at front of work, K1, then K the st from cable needle, rep from * to last 2 sts, K1, P1.
5th row K1, *sl next st onto cable needle and leave at back of work, K1, then P the st from cable needle, K2, sl next st onto cable needle and leave at front of work, P1, then K the st from cable needle, rep from * to last st, K1.
6th row P2, *sl next st onto cable needle and leave at front of work, P1, then K the st from cable needle, sl next st onto cable needle and leave at back of work, K1, then P the st from cable needle, P2, rep from * to end.
These 6 rows form the patt. Cont in patt until work measures 27½in (70cm) from beg, ending with a WS row.
Shape shoulders
Bind off 11[12:13:14] sts at beg of next 6 rows. Cut off yarn and leave rem 62 sts on a holder.

Left front
Using No. 5 (4mm) needles cast on 62[66:74:78] sts. Beg patt.
1st row P1, *K2, P2, rep from * to last 5 sts, K5.
2nd row K6, *P2, K2, rep from * to end.
Rep these 2 rows until work measures

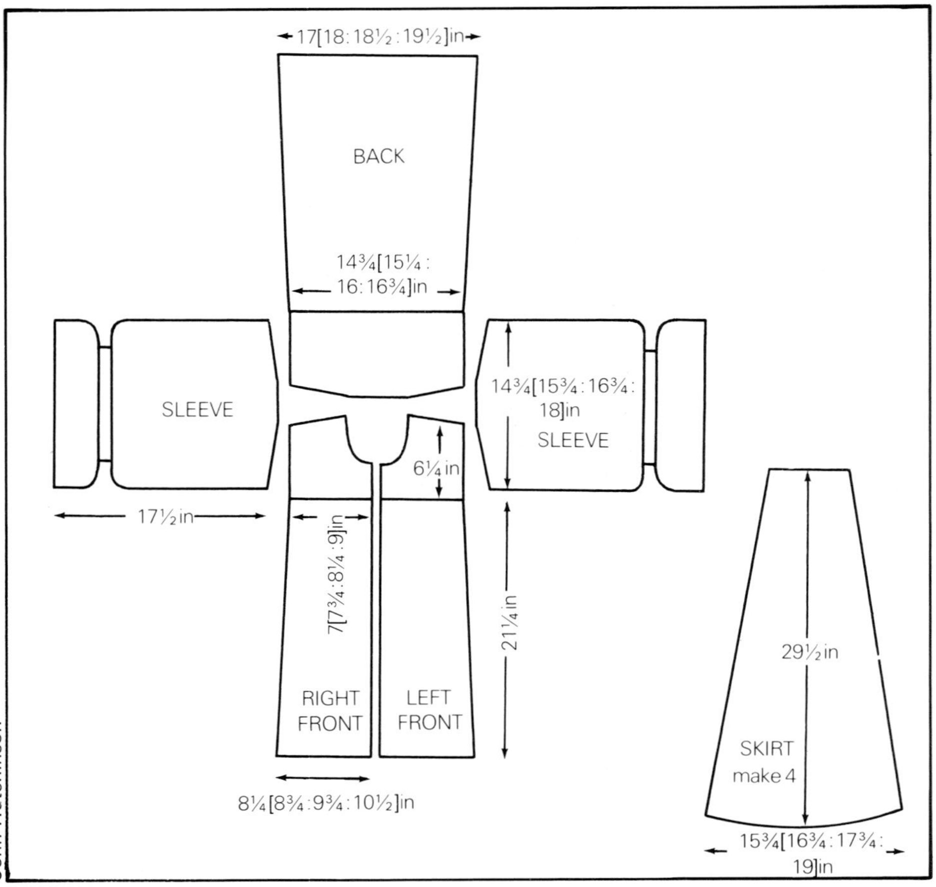
17[18:18½:19½]in
BACK
14¾[15¼:16:16¾]in
SLEEVE
17½in
6¼in
7[7¾:8¼:9]in
21¼in
14¾[15¾:16¾:18]in
SLEEVE
RIGHT FRONT
LEFT FRONT
8¼[8¾:9¾:10½]in
29½in
SKIRT make 4
15¾[16¾:17¾:19]in
John Hutchinson

21¼in (54cm) from beg, ending with a 2nd row and dec one st at end of last row on 1st and 3rd sizes and inc one st on 2nd and 4th sizes. 61 [67:73:79] sts. Cut off yarn and leave sts on a spare needle.

Yoke edging

Using No. 2 (3mm) needles cast on 55[61:67:73] sts. K 11 rows.

Join yoke edging to front by placing WS of yoke edging to RS of front and using No. 2 (3mm) needles K one st from front, *K one st from front tog with one st from yoke edging, rep from * to last 5 sts on front, K5. 61 [67:73:79] sts.

Next row K to end.

Next row P3, *K2, P4, rep from * to last 10 sts, K2, P3, K5.

Cont 5-st garter st border at front edge, cont in patt as for back yoke—i.e. 1st row will read K8, *sl next st onto cable needle and leave at back of work, P1, then P the st from cable needle, K4, rep from * to end, but finish last rep K3 instead of K4—until work measures 3¼in (8cm) less than back to shoulder shaping, ending at side edge.

Shape neck

Next row Patt 49[53:57:61], turn and leave rem sts on a holder.

**Dec one st at neck edge on the next 16[17:18:19] rows. 33[36:39:42] sts. Cont straight until work measures same as back to shoulder; end at side edge.

Shape shoulder

Bind off 11 [12:13:14] sts at beg of next and foll alternate row. Work 1 row. Bind off.

Right front

Using No. 5 (4mm) needles cast on 62[66:74:78] sts. Beg patt.

1st row K5, *K2, P2, rep from * to last st, K1.

2nd row K2, *P2, K2, rep from * to last 4 sts, K4.

Rep these 2 rows until work measures 21¼in (54cm) from beg; end with a 2nd row and dec one st at beg of last row on 1st and 3rd sizes and inc one st on 2nd and 4th sizes. 61 [67:73:79] sts. Cut off yarn and leave sts on a spare needle.

Yoke edging

Using No. 2 (3mm) needles cast on 55[61:67:73] sts. K 11 rows. Join yoke edging to front by placing WS of yoke edging to RS of front and using No. 2 (3mm) needles K 5 sts from front, *K one st from front tog with one st from yoke edging, rep from * to last st on front, K1. 61 [67:73:79] sts.

Next row K to end.

Next row K5, P3, *K2, P4, rep from * to end, but finish last rep, P3 instead of P4. Cont the 5-st garter st border at front edge, cont in patt as for back yoke—i.e. 1st row will read K3, *sl next st onto cable needle and leave at back of work, P1, then P the st from cable needle, K4, rep from * to last 4 sts, K4—until front measures 3¼in (8cm) less than back to shoulder shaping, ending at front edge.

Shape neck

Next row Patt 12[14:16:18], sl these sts onto a holder, patt to end of row. Work as left front from ** to end.

Sleeves

Using No. 5 (4mm) needles cast on 110[118:126:134] sts. Work the 2 main patt rows of back for 4in (10cm), ending with a 1st row.

Next row K2, *P2 tog, K2, rep from * to end. 83[89:95:101] sts. Change to No. 2 (3mm) needles. K19 rows.

Next row K2, *inc in next st, K2, rep from * to end. 110[118:126:134] sts. Change to No. 5 (4mm) needles and beg with a 1st patt row, cont in patt until sleeve measures 17½in (44cm) from beg.

Shape top

Bind off 10[11:12:13] sts at beg of next 10 rows. Bind off.

Neckband and collar

Join shoulder seams. With RS facing place right front sts from holder onto a No. 2 (3mm) needle, then onto same needle pick up and K 30 sts along right front neck, K back neck sts from holder, pick up and K 30 sts along left front, K left front sts. 146[150:154:158] sts. K 11 rows. Change to No. 5 (4mm) needles and cont in patt as for back for 2¼in (6cm). Bind off.

Ties (make 2)

Using No. 2 (3mm) needles cast on 150 sts. K11 rows. Bind off.

To finish

With center of sleeve cap to shoulder seam, sew sleeves to back and fronts. Join side and sleeve seams. Sew on ties.

Skirt

Panels (make 4)

Using No. 5 (4mm) needles cast on 118[126:134:142] sts.

1st row P1, *K2, P2, rep from * to last st, K1.

2nd row K2, *P2, K2, rep from * to end.

Rep these 2 rows until work measures 10¾in (27cm) from beg; end with a 2nd row. Change to No. 4 (3¾mm) needles and cont in patt until work measures 18½in (47cm) from beg; end with a 2nd row. Change to No. 3 (3¼mm) needles for yoke.

Next row P1, *K2 tog, P2 tog, rep from * to last st, K1.

Cont in single ribbing until work measures 28¼in (72cm); end with WS row. Change to No. 2 (3mm) needles and rib 1¼in (3cm). Bind off in ribbing.

To finish

Join seams. Work a herringbone casing over elastic at waist.

SEWING

Made with loving care

This exquisite christening gown is inspired by a Victorian petti-coat design. The basic shape is very simple, but the pretty tucks and delicate trimming make this dress a family treasure.

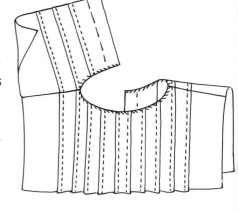

Measurements
To fit ages 3-6 months.
Finished length 33in (84cm).
$\frac{5}{8}$in (1.5cm) seam allowances and 2$\frac{1}{2}$in (6.5cm) hem allowance have been included throughout.
Note French seams are used throughout.

Suggested fabrics
Lawn, chambray or voile for the summer; a wool/cotton blend or lightweight pure wool for winter.

Materials
2$\frac{1}{8}$yd (1.9m) of 36in (90cm)-wide fabric; if using sheer fabric and lining gown, 4$\frac{1}{4}$yd (3.8m) of 36in (90cm)-wide fabric (see page 103)
Matching thread
5yd (4.5m) of $\frac{3}{8}$in (1cm)-wide satin ribbon
2$\frac{1}{4}$yd (2m) of $\frac{1}{4}$in (6mm)-wide satin ribbon
2$\frac{3}{4}$yd (2.5m) of $\frac{5}{8}$in (1.5cm)-wide lace or eyelet for threading with ribbon
2$\frac{1}{2}$yd (2.2m) of $\frac{3}{4}$in (2cm)-wide lace or eyelet edging
2$\frac{1}{4}$yd (2m) of 1$\frac{5}{8}$in (4cm)-wide lace or eyelet edging
Two $\frac{3}{8}$in (1cm)-diameter buttons
Cotton embroidery floss (optional)
Flexible curve, yardstick, tailor's chalk, pencil, paper for pattern

Making the yoke
The tucked yoke sections are prepared before the pattern pieces are cut out.
1 For front yoke, cut a piece of fabric 15$\frac{3}{4}$ by 5$\frac{1}{2}$in (40 by 14cm). For back yoke, cut two pieces each 8 by 5$\frac{1}{2}$in (20 by 14cm).
2 Mark tuck lines on the yoke pieces as indicated. These lines are the stitching lines. Fold halfway between the first pair of lines, wrong sides together and sew through both layers of fabric to form a $\frac{3}{16}$in (5mm) tuck. Repeat for other tucks. Press each group of tucks outward.
3 Cut out paper patterns for the front and back yoke sections. Fold front yoke, matching tucks. Pin pattern piece on fabric and cut out. For the back yoke, pin the two pieces of fabric together around edges, matching tucks. Position pattern piece over yoke pieces and cut out.

4 Sew front yoke to back yokes at shoulders. Fold under and baste 1$\frac{1}{8}$in (3cm)-wide facings at center back, finishing the edges. Overcast the neck edge.
5 Cut two 8in (20cm) and one 3$\frac{1}{8}$in (8cm) pieces of eyelet for threading and insert corresponding pieces of ribbon. Topstitch the short piece between the tucks on the center front yoke. Topstitch the longer pieces close to armholes over shoulders. Cut two 4in (10cm) pieces of ribbon and sew in place between second and third tuck, on each side of center front. Sew one edge of ribbon only, stitching close to tuck stitching line.
6 Cut a piece of $\frac{5}{8}$in (1.5cm)-wide lace edging to fit around neck edge, adding 1$\frac{1}{8}$in (3cm) allowance at each end. With raw edges even, sew edging around neck. Finish edges.

Measurement diagram

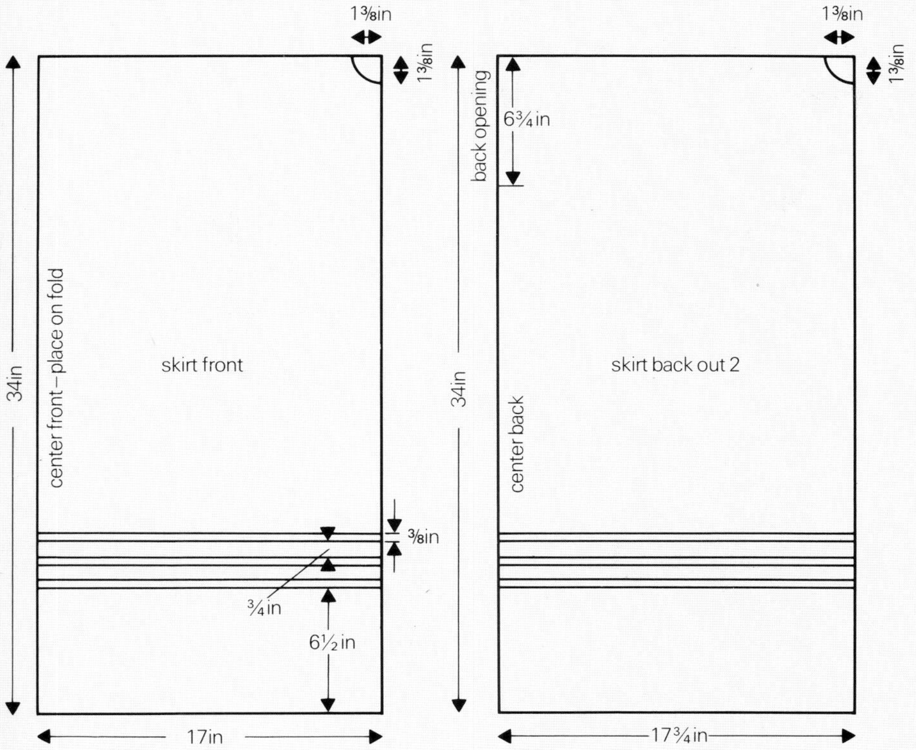

Cutting layout

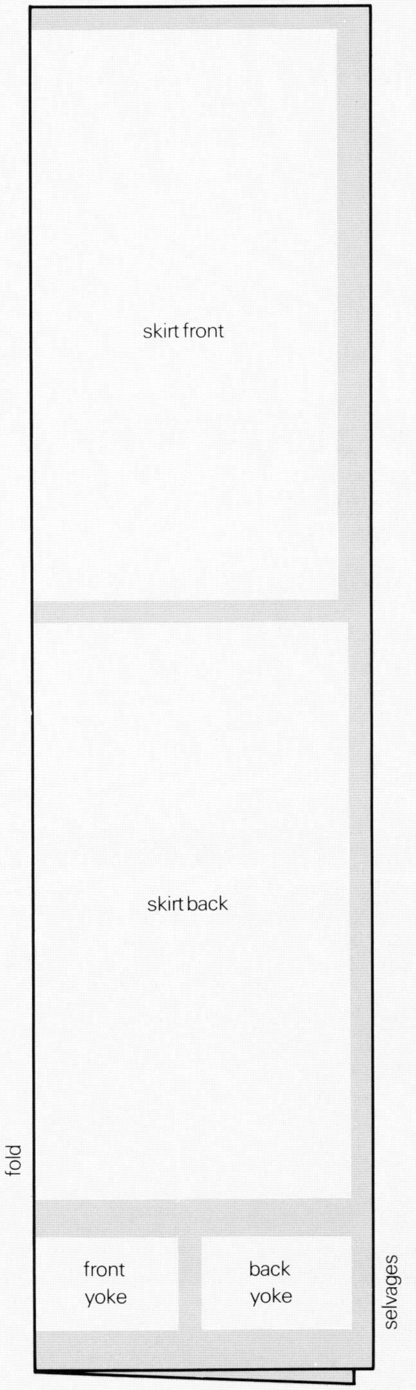

skirt front

skirt back

front yoke

back yoke

fold

selvages

1⅜in

1⅜in

1⅜in

1⅜in

1⅜in

back opening

6¾in

34in

skirt front

center front – place on fold

34in

skirt back out 2

center back

⅜in

¾in

6½in

17in

17¾in

Yoke pattern pieces

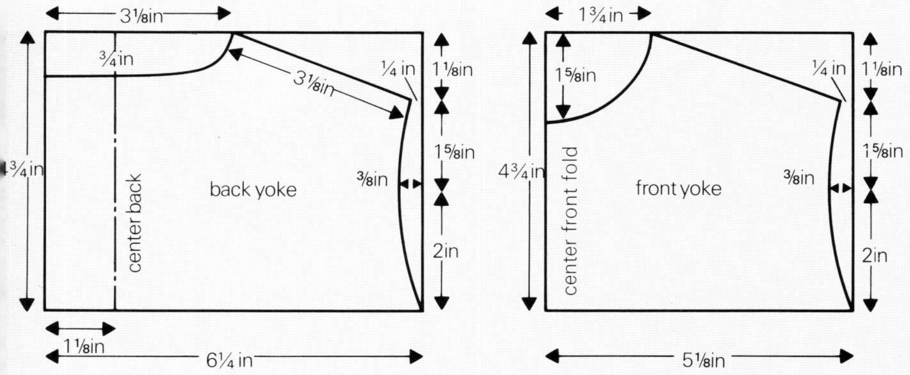

3⅛in

¾in

3⅛in

¼in

1⅛in

1⅝in

⅜in

2in

4¾in

back yoke

center back

1⅛in

6¼in

1¾in

1⅝in

¼in

1⅛in

1⅝in

⅜in

2in

4¾in

front yoke

center front fold

5⅛in

Tucks for yoke pieces

tucks

⅜in 5⅛in ⅜in 5⅛in ⅜in 5⅛in ⅜in 5⅛in 1in ⅜in 5⅛in ⅜in 5⅛in ⅜in 5⅛in ⅜in 5⅛in ⅜in

center front

front yoke

5½in

15¾in

tucks

2½in

⅜in 5⅛in ⅜in 5⅛in ⅜in 5⅛in ⅜in

back yoke

5½in

8in

101

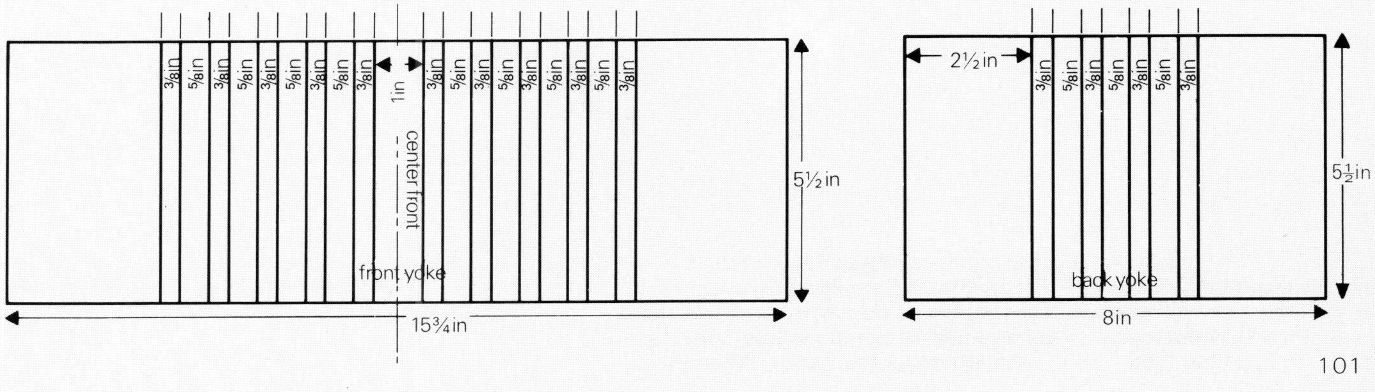

Making the skirt

1 Measure and cut out the back and front skirt sections, following the measurement diagram. Place center front on fold of fabric. Cut two back pieces. Use flexible curve to draw in underarm shape. Mark lines for three horizontal tucks, each $\frac{3}{16}$in (5mm) deep as shown. Mark center back opening.

2 Sew side seams of skirt and center back seam as far as opening.

3 Turn up and sew a $2\frac{1}{2}$in (6.5cm) hem. Make three horizontal tucks, $\frac{3}{16}$in (5mm) deep, around hem of robe in positions marked. Cut 67in (170cm) pieces of $\frac{3}{4}$in (2cm) edging, $1\frac{5}{8}$in (4cm) edging and $\frac{5}{8}$in (1.5cm) eyelet. Cut two 67in (170cm) pieces of ribbon; thread one through eyelet.

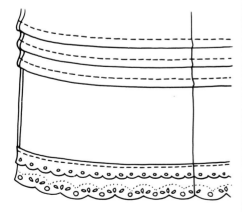

4 Pin and baste the wider edging around the hem, starting from the center back seam, so that the edge just covers the hem of the dress. Pin and baste the narrower edging on top, raw edges even, so that it overlaps as shown. Turn under and join ends of edging at center back. Stitch through the top edges of the two pieces.

5 Pin and baste one piece of ribbon over the raw edges of the edging. Sew on upper edge only, finishing the ends as before.

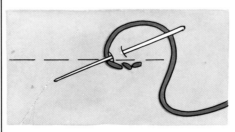

6 Thread the remaining piece of ribbon through the eyelet. Pin, baste and sew in place above ribbon so that the hem stitching is covered, finishing ends as before.

7 Work 2 rows of feather stitch around the skirt, between the top of the hem and the first pin tuck (see Technique tip).

Joining up and finishing

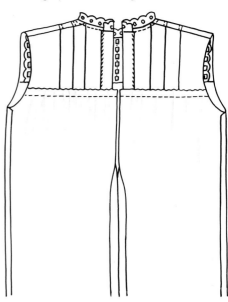

1 Run two lines of gathering stitches around top edge of skirt. Pull up threads until skirt fits lower edge of yoke. Pin yoke to skirt, right sides together and raw

Technique tip
Feather stitch

Mark the positions of the two lines of feather stitch with lines of basting. The stitch is worked on the right side of the fabric, from right to left. Secure the thread with a tiny backstitch on the wrong side of the fabric, on the line of basting.

needle over the marked line and looping the thread around it.

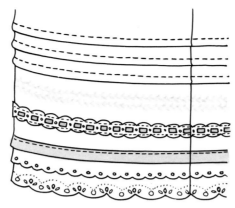

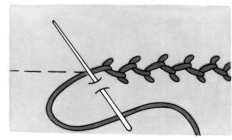

Bring the needle to the right side of the fabric. Take a small stitch diagonally above and to the right, bringing the

Make the second stitch below the line, taking a small diagonal stitch and looping the thread around the needle as before. The stitches should be about $\frac{1}{8}$in (3mm) apart, $\frac{1}{16}$in (1-2mm) away from the marked line, on alternate sides of it.

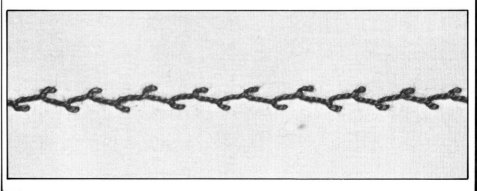

edges even, distributing gathers evenly.
Baste and sew in place. Press seam
allowances up.

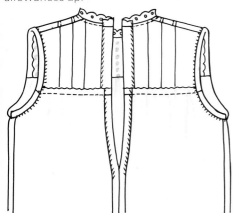

2 Sew a $\frac{1}{4}$in (6mm) hem around armholes
and center back opening from the waist
downward. Make two buttonholes, one
$\frac{3}{4}$in (2cm) from top of bodice and the
other 2in (5cm) below that, on right-hand
side of bodice opening. Sew two
buttons to left-hand side to match.

3 Sew two $\frac{1}{4}$in (6mm)-wide ribbons,
each about 40in (1m) long, on both
sides of front at base of yoke; tie in a bow.

Note
If you are using a transparent fabric it
will be necessary to line the gown. In this
case, double the quantity of fabric
required and make the lining without
decoration.
Prepare the tucking for the yoke as
described and cut out. Then cut out a
second, plain yoke. Baste yoke and lining
together and then treat as one piece
of fabric.
For the skirt, cut out a second skirt from
lining fabric and sew side and center
back seams. Slip lining inside skirt with
wrong sides together and baste along
top edge. Gather up and sew to yoke in
one with the top layer. Hem the lining
separately, making a $3\frac{1}{8}$in (8cm)-deep
hem.

Terry Evans

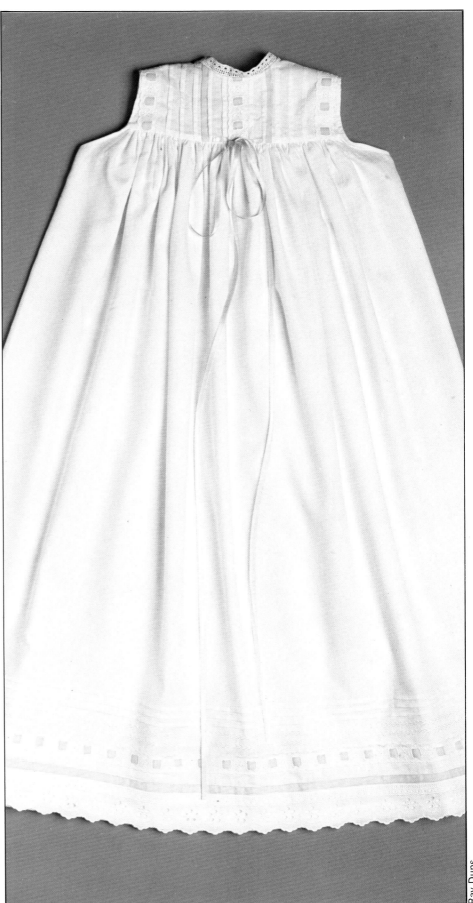

Ray Duns

103

SEWING

Skirts with a swing

Ultra-simple circular skirts for vacations or leisure wear. For extra fun, decorate the hemline with colorful appliqués or rows of bright, contrasting braid.

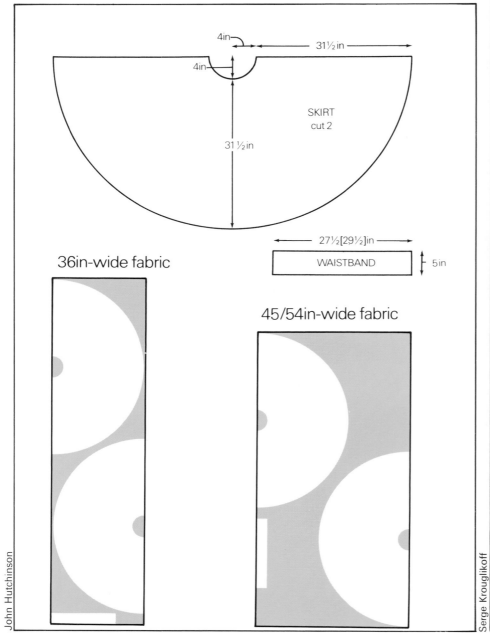

4in

4in

31½ in

SKIRT
cut 2

31 ½ in

27½[29½]in

WAISTBAND

5in

36in-wide fabric

45/54in-wide fabric

John Hutchinson

Serge Krouglikoff

Measurements
To fit sizes 12 and 14.
Finished skirt length: 30⅜in (77cm).

Note Directions are given for size 12, with size 14 in brackets []. If there is only one measurement, it applies to both sizes.

Suggested fabrics
For everyday wear, make the skirt in cotton, fine wool, synthetics or blends. For extra sparkle, make the skirt in satin or taffeta. Corduroy, velvet and one way designs are not recommended.

Materials
- 36in (90cm)-wide fabric: 4yd (3.6m)
- 45in (115cm)-wide fabric 3⅝yd (3.3m)
- 54in (150cm)-wide fabric: 3¼yd (2.9m)
- 6in (15cm) zipper
- 1yd (1m) waistband interfacing 2½in (6cm) wide
- Soft pencil or crayon, fine string or strong thread, thumbtack
- 16 ready-made appliqués (optional)
- 7¾yd (7m) each yellow and blue braid for trim (optional)

Cutting out
1 Lay fabric on cutting surface. Measure and mark a point 35½in (90cm) down one selvage. Tie one end of string to a thumb tack. Attach a pencil to the thread so that it is 35½in (90cm) from pin. Stick thumb tack into selvage at marked point and draw semi-circle.
2 Repeat down the opposite side of the fabric, making the second semi-circle so that the circumferences just meet.
3 Repeat the process, marking a 4in (10cm)-diameter circle at waist of each section as shown in measurement diagram. Cut out the skirt pieces.
4 Cut waistband from remaining fabric.
5 Cut waistband interfacing same length as waistband but half the width.

Making up
1 Join side seams, leaving an opening 6½in (16.5cm) long down left-hand side for zipper. Press seams open and finish seam allowances.

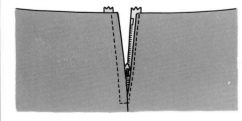

2 Insert zipper by lapped seam method (see Volume 2, page 45).
3 Run a line of gathering stitches, by hand or machine, around the waist of the skirt.

4 Baste interfacing to wrong side of waistband, matching one long edge of interfacing to the center of the waistband, easing fullness to fit.

5 Fold waistband in half, right sides together, down length of waistband. Stitch short ends of waistband. Press. Grade seam allowances and trim corners. Turn waistband right side out.

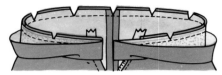

6 Pin the interfaced edge of the waistband to the skirt, right sides together. Starting from the front of the skirt, match end of waistband to edge of zipper, lapping edges. Pin the waistband in place around the skirt, easing the fullness into the waistband. Clip into seam allowance of skirt to line of gathering stitches so that skirt lies flat in the waistband.

7 Baste and machine stitch in place. Press seams and grade seam allowances.

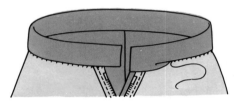

8 Turn band and press upward. Turn in seam allowance along free edge of waistband. Press. Slip stitch in place, slip stitching both raw edges together along underlap.

9 Attach hooks and eyes at waist to fasten.

10 Try on skirt and check length. If the fabric is fairly loosely woven, leave the skirt to hang for a few days before final fitting. Trim hemline if necessary. The hem should not be more than $\frac{5}{8}$in (1.5cm) deep. Turn up hem, easing extra fullness around the skirt (see Technique tip).

Decorative touches

To emphasize the fullness of the skirt, the hemline may be decorated with appliquéd motifs or braid. The extra weight gives the skirt added "swing."

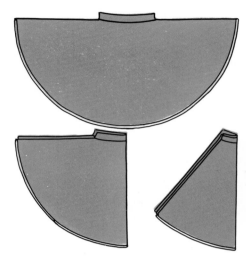

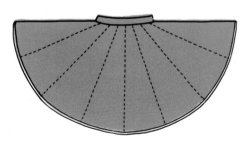

1 For appliquéd motifs, cut out 16 simple shapes or use purchased motifs. Mark the positions for the motifs by folding the skirt: fold in half flat, then fold again so that you have a quarter circle. Fold in half twice more: mark each foldline as the position of a motif.

2 Pin and baste motifs in place around hem of skirt, positioning them 3in (7.5cm) from the lower edge. Topstitch in position, or slip stitch by hand.

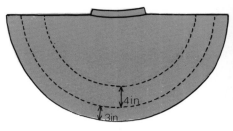

3 For a braid trim, mark two lines of basting stitches around hem of skirt, 3in (7.5cm) and 7in (17.5cm) from finished hemline. Pin braid around hem of skirt in wide, zig-zag stripes. On this skirt, two contrasting bands of braid are used.

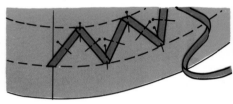

4 Starting from one seamline, pin the first color in position $\frac{5}{8}$in (1.5cm) from hemline, with the raw end turned under. Pin in position at an angle of about 45° to the seamline. When you reach the second line of basting, turn the braid down, pinning it so that it lies at right angles to itself.

5 Continue around the skirt to make a zig-zag pattern. Turn under end. Adjust angle of zig-zags if necessary so that ends meet neatly.

6 Repeat the process with the second color braid, positioning it $\frac{3}{8}$in (1cm) above the first piece and parallel to it, turning under ends as before.

7 Baste braid in place, then machine stitch.

Technique tip

Taking in fullness in a flared hem

When you pin up a flared or circular hem, you will find that folds appear on the upper edge of the hem. There are various ways of eliminating these folds, depending on the type of fabric used.
The first point is to turn up as small a hem as possible. Start by measuring an marking the hemline in the usual way (see Volume 1, page 50). Trim the hem to $\frac{5}{8}$in-$\frac{3}{4}$in (1.5-2cm) from the marked line.

If the fabric can be shrunk (this method is generally applied to wool fabrics) the fullness can be eased by pressing. Run a line of gathering stitches around top of hem, $\frac{1}{4}$in (6mm) from upper edge. Draw up threads so that fullness is taken in. Place a cloth or sheet of paper between skirt and hem and press gently with the tip of a steam iron or dry iron with a

damp cloth. This will shrink away the fullness. Leave to dry, then finish edges with binding, hand overcasting or zig-zag stitching. Sew hem in place by blind stitching.

If the fabric will not shrink, pin the fullness into tiny pleats all around skirt. Hem by slip stitching, securing the pleats with back stitches.

Homemaker

Roll up

Here is a simple way to keep your jewelry safe and neat—in a pretty, quilted fabric roll. It's perfect for traveling too.

Materials
 Tracing paper
 Thin cardboard
 ¼yd (.2m) of 36in (90cm)-wide quilted cotton print fabric
 ⅜yd (.3m) of 36in (90cm)-wide plain fabric
 Bias binding in contrasting color
 Matching and contrasting thread
 6in (15cm) zipper, two small snaps
 ¾yd (.7m) of narrow decorative cord
 Small scraps of felt in three different colors to match fabric
 Small amount of thick knitting yarn
 Large bodkin

Note ⅜in (1cm) seam allowances have been included throughout.

Cutting layout : quilted fabric

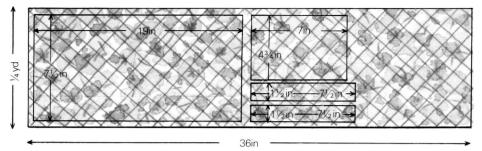

Cutting layout : plain fabric

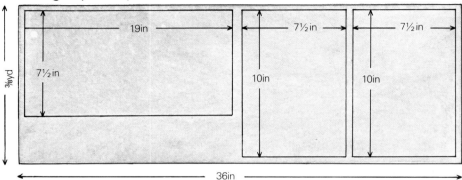

1 From quilted fabric (top) cut one piece 19 × 7½in (48 × 19cm) for outside of roll; two strips, each 7½ × 1½in (19 × 4cm) for ring holders and one piece 7 × 4¾in (18 × 12cm) for brooch pad.
2 From plain fabric (above) cut one piece 19 × 7½in (48 × 19cm) to line the inside of the roll and two pieces each 10 × 7½in (25 × 19cm) for pockets.

3 Trace the flower motif, mark on thin cardboard and carefully cut out. Mark around flower pattern three times on each of the different colored felts. Cut out the nine flowers.

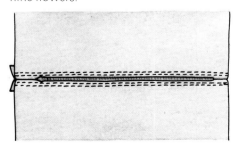

4 Join the two pocket pieces, right sides together, for ¾in (2cm) at each end of

short sides. Insert the zipper in the opening by the slot seam method (see Volume 4, page 68), using two rows of stitching.
5 Place the wrong side of this pocket piece on the right side of the large fabric lining piece. Pin and baste together.

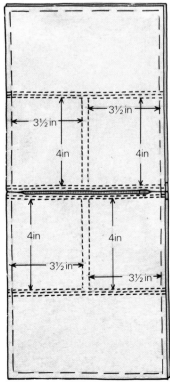

6 Following the diagram and using contrasting thread, make two double

rows of topstitching to divide the fabric up into four sections, with middle sections 4in (10cm) deep. Add single rows of topstitching down the middle of the two center panels and close to the existing rows of double topstitching, to make four small pockets measuring 4 × 3½in (10 × 9cm).

7 Turn under seam allowance all around brooch pad; pin and baste along folded edge. Pin and baste the pad on one of the end sections made by the topstitching. Topstitch the brooch pad in place with two rows of stitches close to edge.

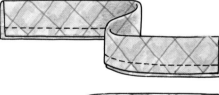

8 Fold each ring holder in half lengthwise with right sides together. Pin, baste and sew long edges. Turn each holder right side out. Press so the seam runs down center.

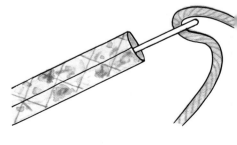

9 Using a yarn needle, thread strands of thick yarn through each holder until softly padded.
10 Turn in the edges at one end of each holder and slip stitch the folded edges together neatly in order to close them.

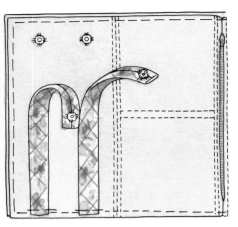

11 Pin and baste the opposite end of each holder onto one long edge of plain fabric, spacing them evenly at the end opposite the brooch pad.

12 Sew half of a snap to the free end of each holder and opposite halves to plain fabric to correspond.

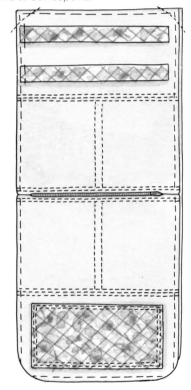

13 Pin the quilted outside piece and the plain inside piece together, with wrong sides facing. Trim the fabric carefully around each corner point to form neat curves. Pin and baste around the outer edge through both layers.

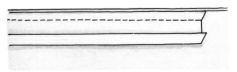

14 Open one side of the binding and pin it to the plain fabric, with right sides

together and raw edges even. Baste along the binding crease. Cut off extra binding, leaving enough for joining. Sew the short ends together and finger-press the seams. Now carefully sew the binding in place along the crease.

15 Fold binding over raw edge to outside (quilted side); pin and baste. Slip stitch in place.

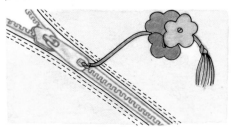

16 Tie a piece of cord $2\frac{1}{2}$in (6.5cm) long to zipper pull. Knot end and unravel below knot to form tiny tassel. Sew three flowers, one of each color, to cord.

17 Sew the center of the remaining piece of cord to the center of the outer bound edge at the brooch pad end of the roll. Make small tassels and decorate cord ends with flowers as on zipper cord.

18 Roll up the bag, starting at the ring holder, and tie the cord around it.

Homemaker

More light on lampshades

These cone-shaped lampshades are surprisingly easy to make. All you need for the frame is a couple of lampshade rings or an old lampshade. For the cover use fabric or wallpaper to complement your decorating scheme.

Kim Sayer

Kim Sayer

Plain cone-shaped lampshade

Materials

Note The materials given here will make a 10in (25cm) tall lampshade, with a 4¾in (12cm) diameter top and 11¾in (30cm) diameter base.

> One plastic-coated lampshade ring
>   with finial ring, 4¾in (12cm) in
>   diameter
> One plain plastic-coated lampshade
>   ring 11¾in (30cm) in diameter (or
>   use the rings from an old
>   lampshade)
> 3⅞yd (3.5m) of ⅜in (1cm)-wide white
>   cotton tape
> Transparent tape
> ¾yd (.6m) of 48in (122cm)-wide
>   fabric and 24in (60cm) of 36in
>   (92cm)-wide stiff paper
> Cardboard tube
> Clothespins
> Clear fabric adhesive
> Spray adhesive
> White thread
> 1⅝yd (1.4m) of trimming
> Plain or graph paper for pattern
> Sharp scissors, ruler, pencil
> Large compass (optional)

1 Tape the two lampshade rings. On the plain ring, start the taping by sticking the end of the cotton tape to the ring with transparent tape.

2 Wind the tape evenly around the ring, at an angle, pulling the tape as you work, so it fits around the ring smoothly.

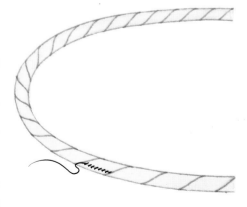

3 To finish, cut off excess tape; turn under the raw end and sew it to the outside of the taped ring, using small stitches.

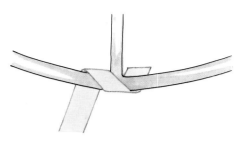

4 On the ring that fits onto the lamp, start the taping at one strut; wrap the tape over the end as shown. Continue winding the tape evenly around the ring, as for the plain ring. To finish, work around to first strut and stitch, as for plain ring.

5 Measure the diameter and circumference of each ring.

6 Decide on the depth of the lampshade; as a guide, clamp a strip of paper to the two rings, using clothespins, and alter the length until it looks correct.

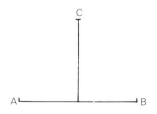

7 Make a paper pattern. On a piece of plain or graph paper, draw a straight horizontal line AB, the length being the diameter of the base ring. Mark the center point of this line.

8 Draw a line up from this center point, at right angles to AB, and the depth of the finished frame, C.

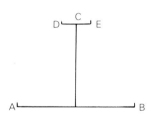

9 Draw another horizontal line, parallel to AB, with point C as the center. Make this line, DE, as long as the diameter of the top ring.

10 Join up points AD and BE, continuing the lines until they cross (point F).

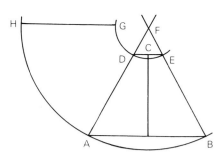

11 Now draw two arcs, the first one with a radius of FE, and the second FB. (Use a large compass, or a tape measure with an eyelet at one end and a pencil inserted in the eyelet, or a piece of string tied around a pencil). Place the compass point at F, and draw arc FE, continuing the arc, EG, out at one side of the triangle, until it measures the circumference of the top ring. Repeat for arc FB, continuing line BH, until it measures the circumference of the base ring.

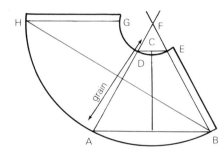

12 This forms the pattern. Now add $\frac{3}{4}$in (2cm) seam allowance to each straight edge.

13 To establish the grain line for the shade, join up HB, find the center point and join this point with F.

14 Cut out the pattern carefully and fix it to the top and base rings using clothespins. Check that it fits correctly and alter if necessary.

15 Carefully bond the fabric to the paper or fabric stiffener before cutting out the shape. Lay the stiffener right side down on a flat surface. Roll the fabric, wrong side out, around a cardboard tube (such as the inside of an aluminum foil roll). As you peel off the protective layer of the stiffener, roll the fabric over the adhesive layer so they stick together without bubbling. If using ordinary stiff paper,

first apply spray adhesive, following the manufacturer's instructions. Unroll fabric as already described.

16 Mark around the pattern and cut out the shape.

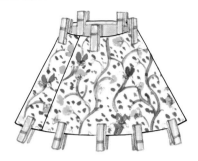

17 Clamp the stiffened fabric around the two rings, using the clothespins.

18 To attach the shade to the taped rings, use a strong double thread and blanket

stitch. Work from the right side through both fabric and tape. These stitches will be covered on the right side by the trimming.

19 Start with the base ring, at a point opposite the seam. Work around one side to the seam, then start at the center again and work around the other side. Finish stitching about 2in (5cm) from each straight edge. Take care that the ring and the edge of the fabric are exactly even. Repeat on the top ring.

20 When the fabric has been stitched to both rings, trim the overlap to between $\frac{1}{2}$ and $\frac{3}{4}$in (1.2 and 2cm), cutting a straight edge with scissors. Glue the overlapping edges together with adhesive. Blanket stitch along the overlapped edges at top and bottom.

21 Glue the trimming in place around the stitching at top and base edges, turning under the raw edges to finish at overlap.

Pleated wallpaper lampshade

Kim Sayer

113

Pleated Wallpaper lampshade

Materials

One plastic-coated lampshade ring with finial ring 4¾in (12cm) in diameter
One plain plastic-coated lampshade ring 11¾in (30cm) in diameter
3⅞yd (3.5m) of ⅜in (1cm)-wide white cotton tape
Wallpaper
Leather punch
Crochet cotton in off-white
Ruler, pencil
Double-sided transparent tape or staple gun and staples

1 Tape the rings as described for the cone-shaped lampshade.
2 Measure the circumference of the base ring and double this measurement. Cut a piece of wallpaper to the depth of the shade.

3 On the wrong side of the wallpaper, mark and draw pencil lines 1½in (4cm) apart across the width, keeping the lines parallel and at right angles to long sides.
4 Carefully score along the pencil lines you've drawn with the closed points of a pair of scissors.

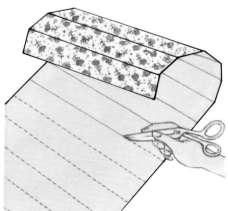

5 Place the first scored line on top of the second scored line and crease the paper again at the fold, to make the first pleat. Each pleat will be ¾in (2cm) deep.

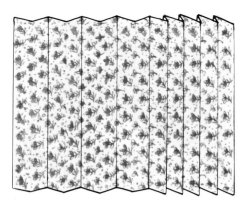

6 Repeat with remaining lines all along the piece of wallpaper.
7 Using the leather punch, make small holes in the center of each pleat, ⅜in (1cm) from outer edge. Repeat to make holes on the lower edge in the same way.
8 Fasten the narrow edges together, using either tape or staples.
9 Thread crochet cotton through the holes along both edges. Spread the pleating around each of the rings in turn. Pull up and tie the ends of crochet cotton.

10 Stitch the pleats to the top ring first. Use a double length of crochet cotton and

work around the ring in a counter-clockwise direction. First attach thread to ring.
11 Push the needle through left-hand hole of first pleat to the right side.
12 Bring the needle back to the wrong side through the hole to the right.

13 Loop the thread under and over ring and push needle through left-hand hole of second pleat.
14 Bring needle to the wrong side again through right-hand hole of the second pleat.
15 Continue, looping thread under and over ring, and pushing needle through left-hand hole of third pleat.
16 When you reach the end of the working thread, pull it up so that the pleats rest against the ring; adjust the pleats evenly and fasten off with a double loop. Re-thread the needle and continue stitching around the ring to the end. (You will need several lengths of thread to complete the stitching.)
17 Repeat for the larger base ring, sewing the pleats to the ring in the same way as before.

Homemaker

Soft fabric frames

Frame your favorite picture with some pretty printed fabric. Or, for an elegant touch, choose a sophisticated satin fabric and add a graceful floral design.

Simple fabric frame

Size
The finished frame measures $10\frac{1}{2} \times 8\frac{1}{2}$in ($27 \times 22$cm) and has an opening of $6\frac{1}{4} \times 4\frac{1}{4}$in ($16 \times 11$cm). You can easily alter the dimensions to suit your picture.

Materials
*Two pieces of print fabric $11\frac{3}{4} \times 10$in
   (30×25cm)*
*Two pieces of strong cardboard
   $10\frac{1}{2} \times 8\frac{1}{2}$in ($27 \times 22$cm)*
$\frac{3}{4}$yd (.7m) of narrow lace
*2yd (1.8m) of $\frac{1}{4}$in (6mm)-wide
   matching ribbon*
*Piece of medium-weight batting
   $10\frac{1}{2} \times 8\frac{1}{2}$in ($27 \times 22$cm)*
Fabric glue, pencil
Matching thread
8in (20cm) of $\frac{3}{8}$in (1cm)-wide elastic
Self-adhesive picture hanger

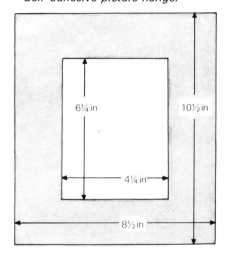

1 Cut a rectangle $6\frac{1}{4} \times 4\frac{1}{4}$in ($16 \times 11$cm) from the center of one piece of cardboard, leaving a frame measuring $2\frac{1}{8}$in (5.5cm) wide on all sides. The second piece will serve as backing.

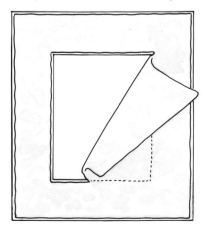

2 Apply fabric glue to one side of cardboard frame, and glue the batting in place on top. When the glue has dried, trim away center section of batting along inner edge of cardboard frame.

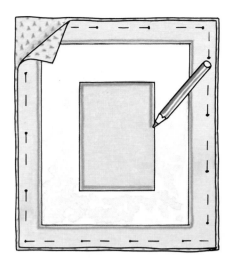

3 Pin the fabric pieces together with right sides facing. Place cardboard frame on fabric, batting upward. Draw around the outer and inner edges of the frame with a pencil. Remove the frame.

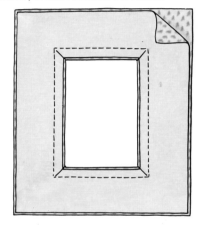

4 Pin, baste and stitch the inner edges of the fabric pieces together. Trim away the center section of the fabric leaving seam allowances of $\frac{1}{4}$in (6mm), and snip into the corners. Turn fabric right side out.

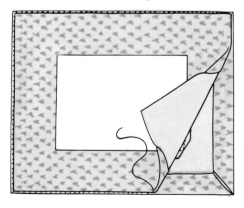

5 Insert padded cardboard frame into fabric frame. Fold outer edges of front fabric over cardboard and glue to back.
6 Turn under raw edges of back so that the fold lies just inside the outer edge of frame. Pin, baste and hand sew over raw edges of front fabric.

Terry Evans

Gary Warren

116

7 Cut lace into four strips to fit the inner edges of the frame. Pin, baste and slip stitch the lace along the inner edges (or glue it in place with fabric glue).

8 Pin, baste and slip stitch the ribbon around the inner edge of frame over the plain edge of the lace, mitering the corners.

9 Cut the elastic into two lengths and pin in place on the back of the frame diagonally across two corners, as shown. Trim the ends to align with the edge of the frame and firmly hand sew these edges in place.

10 Center the picture on the piece of backing cardboard and lay the frame over it. Adjust the position of the picture if necessary, then glue the upper edge to the backing card. Glue a picture-hanger in place on back of card.

11 Slip the mounted picture under the elastic to hold it in place.

Appliquéd satin frame

Size

The finished frame measures $10\frac{1}{2} \times 8\frac{1}{2}$in ($27 \times 22$cm) with an opening $6\frac{1}{4} \times 4\frac{1}{4}$in ($16 \times 11$cm). You can easily alter the dimensions to suit your picture or mirror.

Materials

$\frac{3}{8}$yd (.3m) of 36in (90cm)-wide
   caramel-colored satin
Scraps of dark brown, cream and
   patterned fabric
Pink and brown embroidery thread
   (optional)
Piece of cotton fabric 12×10in
   (30×25cm), for backing
Scraps of thick yarn
Large-eyed needle

Fusible webbing
Piece of medium-weight batting
   $10\frac{1}{2} \times 8\frac{1}{2}$in ($27 \times 22$cm)
$\frac{3}{4}$yd (.6m) of thin filler cord
Piece of strong cardboard $10\frac{1}{2} \times 8\frac{1}{2}$in
   (27×22cm)
Fabric glue
Tracing paper and wheel
Dressmaker's carbon paper
Embroidery hoop, thread
8in (20cm) of $\frac{3}{8}$in (1cm)-wide elastic
Self-adhesive picture hanger

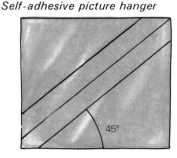

1 From satin cut out two pieces, each 12×8in (30×25cm). From the remaining fabric cut bias strips $\frac{3}{4}$in (2cm) wide; join them on the straight grain and trim to make a strip which is approximately 22in (56cm) long for piping.

2 Make cardboard frame and cover one side with batting as described in steps 1 and 2 on page 116.

3 Center cardboard frame on wrong side of one satin piece. Mark inner and outer edges. Go over the inner edge with a tracing wheel. This will be the frame front.

4 Trace the stems (the long curving lines on the pattern below) on the tracing paper, exactly as they are positioned on the pattern.

5 Using dressmaker's carbon paper and positioning the outline on the frame as shown in the photograph opposite, trace the stem lines onto the right side of the fabric.

6 Cut three strips of fusible webbing, each about 2×7in (5×18cm). Cut two strips each of the dark brown, cream and patterned fabric. Place a strip of webbing between each pair of fabric strips and bond them together following the manufacturer's instructions very carefully.

7 Using dressmaker's carbon and following the key on the pattern, trace the leaves and petals onto the appropriate bonded fabrics, leaving spaces which are roughly equal between them.

8 Cut the motifs apart, but do not actually cut along the lines that you have traced.

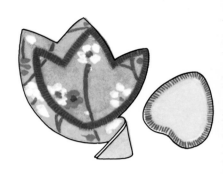

9 Set the machine at a close zig-zag stitch and stitch around the outline of each leaf and petal, using brown and pink thread. Then carefully cut away the excess fabric. Alternatively, you can hand sew the edges, using close blanket stitch and embroidery thread. In this case you should cut along the outlines first.

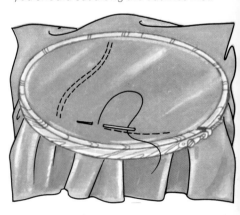

10 Lay the cotton backing fabric on wrong side of frame front. Place both fabrics in an embroidery frame and work back stitch along marked stem lines. Remove fabric from frame. Cut away backing fabric, leaving about $\frac{3}{8}$in (1cm) around the embroidered lines.

KEY

leaves 2,3,6,7,10 – dark brown
   1, 4, 5, 8, 9 – patterned fabric

flower A–D all in cream

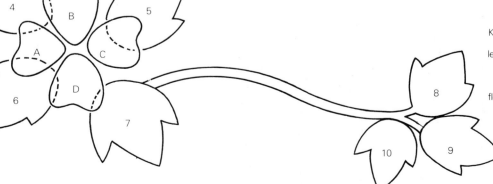

John Hutchinson

11 Thread the needle with a piece of yarn and insert it into one of the channels formed by the double line of stitching on the underside of the frame front. Bring the needle up through the fabric when you can push it no farther, then insert it into the channel again. Continue in this way to the end. Leave ⅜in (2cm) of yarn free at each end of channel. Repeat for other channel. This technique—called Italian quilting—produces a raised line suggesting a stem.

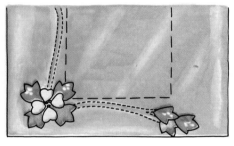

12 Pin, baste and stitch the flower petals and leaves to the frame front in positions marked on the diagram, attaching them only by their base edges.
13 Using pink embroidery floss, work several French knots in the center of the flower to suggest stamens.

14 Pin and baste the piping fabric, right side out, around the cord.

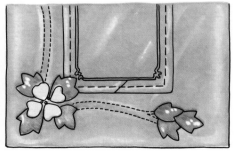

15 Pin and baste the covered piping cord around the marked inner line of the front, with raw edges toward the center.
16 Complete the frame as instructed in steps 4-6 and 9-11 of simple fabric frame. When sewing the inner edges of the frame, take care to hold the leaves and petals out of the way.

Terry Evans

Homemaker

Garden Fresh

If you don't have a green thumb, why not sew your own vegetable pillows? They're conversation pieces and will add a touch of whimsy to any room.

Pumpkin

Materials

$\frac{5}{8}$yd (.5m) of 36in (90cm)-wide
   orange satin
$\frac{1}{2}$yd (.4m) of 36in (90cm)-wide dark
   green satin
Polyester stuffing
Bodkin
Two pipe cleaners
Scraps of lightweight batting
Tracing paper
Dressmaker's carbon paper
Matching thread

1 Trace the patterns for the pumpkin segments, stalk and leaves, but do not cut out the patterns. Using dressmaker's carbon paper, transfer the shapes to the wrong side of the appropriate fabrics, to make as many pieces as indicated on the pattern. Cut out each piece, adding $\frac{3}{8}$in (1cm),seam allowance all around.
2 From remaining dark green satin cut out a 2$\frac{1}{4}$in (6cm) diameter circle for pumpkin center.
3 Cut three leaf sections from the batting, without adding the $\frac{3}{8}$in (1cm) for seams.

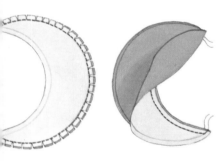

4 Pin, baste and sew the 18 pumpkin segments together. Place them with right sides together and stitch outer and inner curves alternately, leaving an opening in one seam for turning. Clip the curved edges.
5 Turn pumpkin right side out. Stuff it firmly. Turn in opening edges and slip stitch them together.

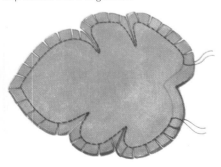

6 Pin, baste and sew the leaves together in pairs, placing right sides together and leaving base edges open. Clip at short intervals around the seam.
7 Turn leaves right side out. Insert batting sections through openings. Turn in opening edges, slip stitch to close.

8 Topstitch down the center of each leaf to represent a vein.

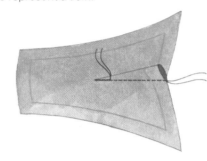

9 Pin, baste and sew the dart in each stalk section.

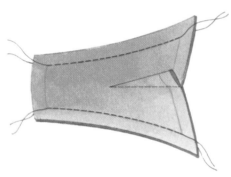

10 Place the two stalk sections with right sides together. Pin, baste and sew side edges of stalk. Turn the stalk right side out.

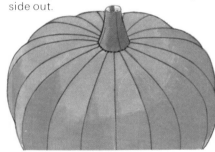

11 Turn under raw edges around base of stalk; pin, baste and slip stitch the folded edge of the stalk to center of one side of pumpkin.
12 Insert stuffing into open end of stalk until it is firm. Turn in remaining open edges of the stalk and slip stitch together to close.

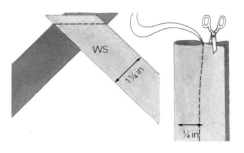

13 For the leaf stems make some green satin tubing, as follows: cut bias strips of fabric 1$\frac{1}{4}$in (3.5cm) wide, joining strips if necessary to make a strip 20in (51cm) long. Join the strips on the straight grain of the fabric, as shown, placing right sides together and raw edges even. Fold the strip in half lengthwise. Pin, baste and sew $\frac{1}{4}$in (6mm) from the folded edge, finishing the stitches by widening the tube slightly at one end, leaving long ends of thread. Trim the seam.

14 Thread the ends of sewing thread into a bodkin and secure ends with a double back stitch. Thread the bodkin through the tube and pull the tube right side out. From the finished tubing cut two pieces, each about 1$\frac{1}{4}$in (3.5cm) longer than the pipe cleaners.

batting

pipe cleaner

15 Roll a layer of batting around each pipe cleaner and insert it into the tubing. Turn in both ends of each tube and slip stitch to close.

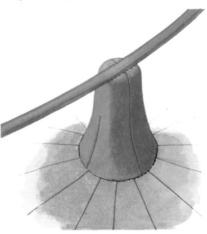

16 Center one stem on top of the free end of the stalk; pin, baste and sew in place.

PUMPKIN LARGE LEAF
cut 4 in dark green

PUMPKIN SMALL LEAF
cut 2 in dark green

PUMPKIN
cut 18 in orange

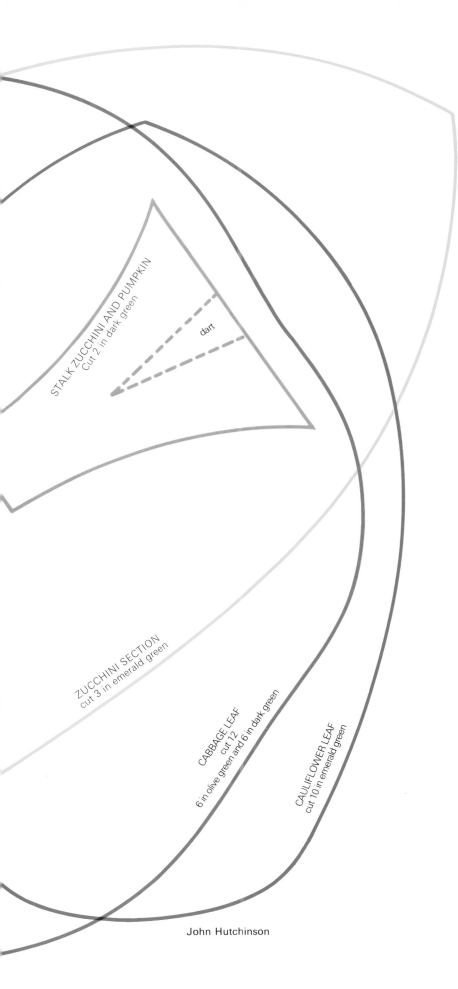

STALK ZUCCHINI AND PUMPKIN
Cut 2 in dark green

dart

ZUCCHINI SECTION
cut 3 in emerald green

CABBAGE LEAF
cut 12
6 in olive green and 6 in dark green

CAULIFLOWER LEAF
cut 10 in emerald green

John Hutchinson

17 Place second stem over the first one so that they are at right angles, matching the centers of the stems. Pin, baste and sew to previously covered pipe cleaner.

18 Pin, baste and sew a leaf to three of the stem ends, as shown, placing the stem on the underside of the leaf.

19 Curl the remaining stem around a pencil to make a curly tendril.

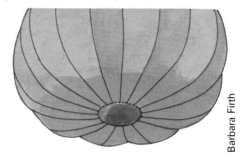

Barbara Firth

20 Turn under the raw edges around the center circle. Pin, baste and sew it in place on the underside of the pumpkin.

123

Cauliflower

Materials

$\frac{5}{8}$yd (.5m) of 36in (90cm)-wide
   ivory satin
$\frac{5}{8}$yd (.5m) of 36in (90cm)-wide
   emerald green satin
20in (50cm) square of scrap fabric,
   such as unbleached muslin
20in (50cm) square of lightweight
   batting
Polyester stuffing
White bedspread mercerized cotton
Large darning needle
Tracing paper and wheel
Dressmaker's carbon paper
String and thumbtack
Pencil and compass
Matching thread

1 Trace the cauliflower leaf pattern.
Using dressmaker's carbon paper, transfer
the leaf shape to the wrong side of the
green satin, as many times as indicated.
Cut out, adding $\frac{3}{8}$in (1cm) for seams.
2 From ivory satin cut out fifteen 7in
(18cm) squares for florets.
3 From batting cut out a piece for each
pair of leaves, without any seam
allowance.

4 On the muslin mark a 19in (48cm)
diameter circle as follows: fold the
muslin square in half; fold in half again
in the opposite direction. Tie one end of a
piece of string around a thumbtack and
the other end around a pencil so that the
string measures 9$\frac{1}{2}$in (24cm). Place the
tack at the point where the folds meet
and draw a curved line from one edge to
the other. Keep string taut as you mark.
Go over line with tracing wheel.

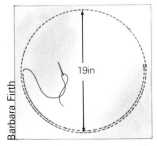

Barbara Firth

5 Hand sew two rows of gathering
around the marked circle. Draw up
gathering threads and fill the center with
stuffing. Pull the threads tight and fasten
off the ends. Cut off excess fabric around
the gathers, leaving $\frac{3}{8}$in (1cm).

6 Mark a 6$\frac{3}{4}$in (17cm) diameter circle on
the right side of each floret square, using
pencil and compass.

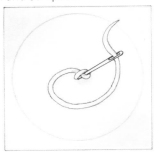

7 Using a darning needle and bedspread
cotton string, make a French knot in the
center of each floret circle, winding the
cotton only once around the needle in
making the knot.

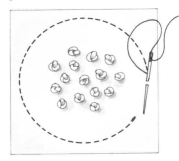

8 Make about 12-14 French knots in the
same way in a group around the central
French knot.
9 Using sewing thread, hand sew a line
of gathering around each marked circle.
Draw up threads and fill each floret with
stuffing, as for muslin foundation ball.
10 Turn muslin foundation ball so that the
smooth side is at the base and the
gathered side is on top.

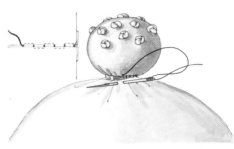

11 Ladder stitch one of the florets to the
gathered (top) side of the foundation
ball, over the tied-up end so that the
floret will be slightly raised.

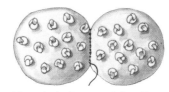

12 Ladder stitch the remaining florets
around the first central floret and then to

each other, so that together they form a
tightly-packed mass.
13 Ladder stitch the outer edges of the
outer ring of florets to the foundation ball.
14 Make the leaves in the same way as
for the pumpkin.

15 Baste the leaves in place around the
foundation ball, overlapping their edges
and leaving a circular gap about 1$\frac{1}{2}$in
(4cm) in diameter at the base. Attach the
bases of the leaves to the ball by hand.
16 Ladder stitch the leaves to the mass of
florets, so that the tops of the leaves are
left free and all the foundation is covered.

17 From remaining emerald green satin
cut out a 3in (8cm) diameter circle. Turn
under $\frac{3}{8}$in (1cm) around edges. Pin,
baste and slip stitch circle to base of
cauliflower, over base ends of leaves.

Cabbage

Materials

$\frac{5}{8}$yd (.5m) of 36in (90cm)-wide
   olive green satin
$\frac{5}{8}$yd (.5m) of 36in (90cm)-wide dark
   green satin
$\frac{5}{8}$yd (.5m) of 36in (90cm)-wide
   emerald green satin
Piece of very pale green satin
   14×6in (35.5×15cm)
20in (50cm) square of cotton fabric,
   such as unbleached muslin
20in (50cm) square of lightweight
   batting
1$\frac{3}{4}$yd (1.5m) of narrow filler cord

124

2¼yd (2m) of thick filler cord
Polyester stuffing; tracing paper;
    dressmaker's carbon paper; thread

Trace the cabbage leaf pattern. Using
dressmaker's carbon paper, mark leaves
on the wrong side of the olive green and
dark green satin. Cut out each leaf,
adding ⅜in (1cm) seam allowance.
From emerald green satin cut out three
pieces, each 20×9in (51×22.5cm).
From batting cut out 6 leaf sections,
without adding ⅜in (1cm) for seams.
Make a muslin foundation ball as for
the cauliflower.

Turn the foundation ball so that the
pale green satin piece is on top. Pin,
baste and slip stitch the pale green satin
over the center of the ball.

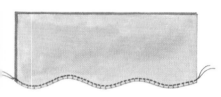

Place two of the emerald green pieces
right sides together. Cut a curved edge
on one long side. Pin, baste and sew
in (1cm) from this edge. Trim seams,
clip edges and turn right side out. Cut
a curved edge on long edge of other
emerald green piece.

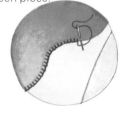

Wrap the single emerald green piece
over the foundation ball so that the curved
edge is toward the center, overlapping
the pale green piece. Blanket stitch along
curved edge. Ladder stitch the remaining
edges in place around foundation ball.

8 Wrap the pair of emerald green pieces
over the foundation ball on the opposite
side, with the curved edge toward the
center, overlapping other two sections.
Ladder stitch outside edges in place.

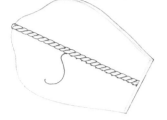

9 Place a piece of thick filler cord down
the center of each batting leaf to represent
a vein. Slip stitch in place.

10 Place two pieces of thin filler cord
at each side of central vein, curving them
out to outer edge. Slip stitch in place.
11 Assemble leaves in the same way as for
pumpkin leaves.

12 After making the leaves, pin, baste
and sew, using a cording foot, down
both sides of thick and thin cord, so that
all the veins show in relief.
13 Baste the dark green leaves to the base
of the foundation ball, overlapping their
edges. Slip stitch in place at the base,
then ladder stitch them to each other and
to the ball so they stand up straight.

14 Baste and hand sew the olive green
leaves to the base of the ball over
previous leaves, overlapping them.

Zucchini

Materials

⅝yd (.5m) of 36in (90cm)-wide
    emerald green satin
Scraps of dark green satin
Pipe cleaner
Polyester stuffing
Jar of fabric paint in
    dark green
Wide paintbrush
Matching thread; tracing
    paper; dressmaker's carbon paper

1 Trace the patterns for the zucchini
section and stalk. Using dressmaker's
carbon paper, mark on the wrong side of
the appropriate fabrics as many pieces as
indicated. Cut out, adding ⅜in (1cm) for
seams.

2 Pin, baste and sew the three zucchini
sections together, right sides facing.
Leave an opening in one seam.
3 Trim seams, clip curves and turn squash
right side out. Stuff firmly. Turn in opening
edges and slip stitch together.

4 Using the fabric paint and a wide brush,
paint stripes along the zucchini.
5 Make the stalk as for pumpkin and sew
it to one end of zucchini.

6 Make one tubing-covered pipe
cleaner in dark green satin, as for
pumpkin. Pin, baste and sew to stalk and
curl it around a pencil.

Homemaker

Tailored tiebacks

For a graceful look, tie back your draperies. You can make tiebacks from matching or contrasting fabric, cut them straight or give them a shape—whichever suits your decor. We give instructions for straight tiebacks trimmed with braid and for scalloped tiebacks; or you can design your own style.

Materials
Fabric to contrast with or match your draperies (see below for amount needed)
Heavyweight iron-on interfacing
Matching thread
Braid (if desired)
1in (2.5cm) diameter curtain rings and hooks

Measuring for tiebacks

1 Width: tiebacks normally measure between 2 and 3in (5 and 8cm) in width, but this is only a guide. Experiment with scraps of fabric and choose a width that looks good in proportion to your draperies. When buying fabric, allow twice the width plus seam allowances.
2 Length: to calculate the length, loop a tapemeasure around the drawn-back curtain at the height you want the tieback to be placed. Adjust it until you find the best length.

Straight tiebacks

1 Measure for tiebacks, as above, and buy the required amount of material and trimmings, if desired.
2 Cut two pieces of fabric, twice the width of the tieback plus 1¼in (3cm) for seams.
3 Cut two pieces of interfacing the exact size of the tiebacks.

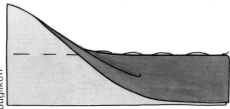

4 Fold each fabric piece in half lengthwise, right sides together, and baste along the foldline.

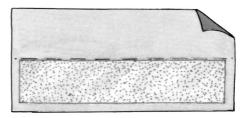

5 Open out each fabric piece and place the interfacing on the wrong side of the tieback, with one long edge to basted line, leaving a ⅝in (1.5cm) margin on the remaining raw edges. Carefully iron interfacing in place.

6 Cut two pieces of braid the same length as the tiebacks. Pin, baste and hand sew each piece of braid to the right side, centering it over the interfaced side of the tieback, excluding the seam allowance.

7 Fold tieback pieces in half lengthwise, with right sides together. Pin, baste and stitch around three sides, taking ⅝in (1.5cm) seams and leaving an opening 2in (5cm) long so that you can turn the tieback right side out.

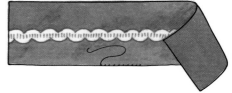

8 Trim seam allowances and cut diagonally across each corner. Turn tiebacks right side out. Turn in opening edges and slip stitch to close.

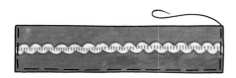

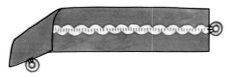

9 Baste around the edge of each tieback, so that the seam is exactly on the outer edge. Press. Remove basting.

10 Sew a curtain ring to the short ends of each tieback with several loose stitches.
11 Screw hooks in place at the side of the windows and loop a tieback around each drape, placing the rings over the hooks.

Shaped tiebacks

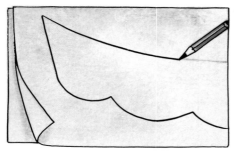

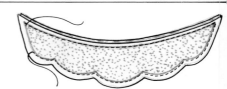

1 Measure for tiebacks, as above and make a paper pattern: first, cut a piece of paper about 4in (10cm) larger all around than the required size and fold the paper in half widthwise, so the resulting pattern will be symmetrical.
2 Draw the shape on one half of the paper, so the central fold of the tieback is on the fold of the paper. To make smoothly curved lines, use a compass or a saucer or small plate. Cut around the shape, still keeping the paper folded in half. Unfold the pattern and slip it around the curtain to check the effect. Adjust the pattern if necessary.

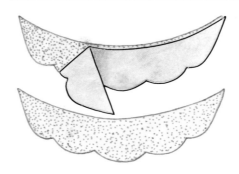

4 From interfacing cut out two tieback pieces, the same size as the pattern.

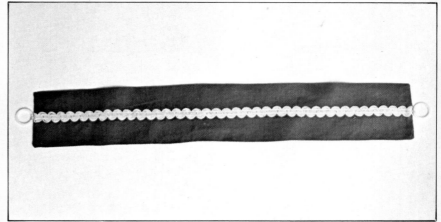

6 Place the interfaced fabric pieces on the other two pieces, right sides together; pin, baste and sew all around, taking $\frac{5}{8}$in (1.5cm) seams and leaving an opening for turning.

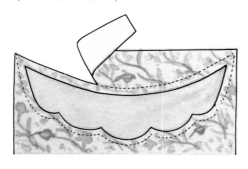

3 Place the fold of the pattern on the straight grain of the fabric and cut out four tieback pieces, adding $\frac{5}{8}$in (1.5cm) for seams all around.

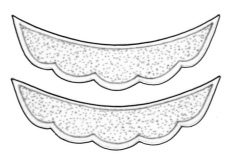

5 Center the interfacing pieces on the wrong side of two fabric pieces, so that there is a $\frac{5}{8}$in (1.5cm) margin all around. Carefully iron interfacing in place.

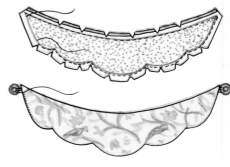

7 Trim seam allowances and clip curves. Turn tiebacks right side out.
Turn in edges along opening and slipstitch to close.
8 Complete and hang as for straight tiebacks.